Praise for *The Happiness Perspective*

"*The Happiness Perspective* is a superb account of positive choices, exercises, and plenty of question to ponder. The book guides its readers to examine their needs and motives for change, and then helps to reveal a path for action. I will be using it soon with my women's groups."

—Barbara Sinor, Ph.D., author, *Finding Destiny*

"Have you ever read a book and had an 'aha' moment where you chuckled out loud or paused and gazed at the sky thinking deeply about what you just read, while completely oblivious to your surroundings? *The Happiness Perspective*, a completely engaging, thought provoking, and easy read did this for me. No tricks or gimmicks or get happy quick schemes. Just good old honest self-examination. At the end of the day, happiness is choice. I had never thought of that before. I was too busy looking, searching, *blah, blah*, for external happiness but it is all internal. From now on, I choose my happiness."

—Annette Sadelson, Rockville, MD

"While much has been written on how to achieve happiness, Diane Wing shines new light on the topic. Diane takes the reader step-by-step through the process of actually shifting one's perspective through all of the layers and circumstances that may comprise the human experience of perceived discontent. *The Happiness Perspective* also teaches how to clear the path of any obstacles that may be in the way. These steps are accomplished not just with the mind, but with the whole self, and from a completely fresh vantage point. Profoundly transformative, *The Happiness Perspective* is a brilliant, comprehensive blueprint for self-awareness, inner peace, and the attainment of ultimate happiness."

—Dyan Garris, author, visionary mystic, and
New Age recording artist

"*The Happiness Perspective: Seeing Your Life Differently* is a guide for living a more positive, productive and healthy life. It shows you how to de-clutter emotional baggage and shows you that you really matter. I enjoyed the very perceptive exercises in the book. They definitely helped me put the focus on what I want and not focusing on what I don't want. Diane's book is truly a stepping stone for the 'aha' moments in life by just changing your perception."

—Donna Phillips, Newark, DE

"When I discovered *The Happiness Perspective,* I was actively acknowledging and releasing negative thoughts and patterns tied to the end of a 30-year professional career. I was surprised to find a comprehensive self-improvement program in this book that succinctly addressed each of my present concerns... as if it was a gift written *just for me.* It provided a perfect roadmap for navigating the realignment of my priorities from corporate to personal abundance and success. I highly recommend it to everyone wanting to release the 'Self that no longer serves you' and embrace the changes that will bring new energy and abundance into their lives."

—Maxine Ashcraft, Oakland, CA

"Diane Wing's style is very easy to read and learn from. I was able to do the exercises and pick up and move on to the next topic. I was generally a happy, go-with-the-flow kind of person. I still am, but with a different perspective on how I look at events in my life. After reading *The Happiness Perspective,* I realized several experiences that I was holding onto were pulling me down when a new and similar experience was happening in my life. I am working through several exercises in this book to let go of the old experiences and learn the lessons my life has for me. I read many books and Ms. Wing's is definitely one that will be kept within easy reach to be read over and over."

—Antoinette Brickhaus, San Diego, CA

"*The Happiness Perspective* is filled with tips and techniques that work to change your worldview and bring calmness into your life. I know because I've tried many of these techniques myself, learning how to do less and enjoy life more."

— Tyler R. Tichelaar, Ph.D. and award-winning author of *The Children of Arthur* series

"In *The Happiness Perspective,* Diane Wing provides powerful, life-changing techniques that are easily incorporated into your daily life. Diane's writing style makes you feel she is speaking directly to you, addressing your specific questions and supporting you during the process. So much has been written about 'happiness', but Diane makes clear that if you're willing to do the work, it can be attained!"

—Maggie Patzuk, Audubon, PA

"I just finished *The Happiness Perspective,* and I really enjoyed it. I am not one for doing exercises in the book but Diane made it easy with how she asks the questions. Also, I feel I could just look up certain situations and learn from it in that moment in time. Thank you for all you do."

—Kathy Sadler, Elkton, MD

"Diane Wing's *The Happiness Perspective* delivers a refreshing message on self awareness and personal development. Life happens... but it's still up to us to manage self. Diane's message is clear; as humans we alone are accountable and responsible for our personal happiness and her 'take charge' approach along with practical techniques such as "grounding" help to navigate. A good read!"

—Sandi Stephenson, Toronto, Canada.

The Happiness Perspective

Seeing Your Life Differently

by Diane Wing, M.A.

Loving Healing Press

Ann Arbor • London • Sydney

Learn more at www.DianeWing.com

Paperback 978-1-61599-320-8
Hardcover 978-1-61599-321-5
eBook 978-1-61599-322-2

Distributed by Ingram (USA/CAN), Bertram's Books (UK/EU), Ingram
International (AU)

Library of Congress Cataloging-in-Publication Data

Names: Wing, Diane, 1959- author.
Title: The happiness perspective : seeing your life differently / by Diane
    Wing, M.A.
Description: 1st Edition. | Ann Arbor : Loving Healing Press, [2016] |
    Includes bibliographical references.
Identifiers: LCCN 2016046961| ISBN 9781615993208 (pbk. : alk. paper) |
ISBN
    9781615993215 (hardcover : alk. paper) | ISBN 9781615993222 (ePub,
PDF,
    Kindle)
Subjects: LCSH: Happiness. | Self-actualization (Psychology) | Mind and
body.
Classification: LCC BF575.H27 W564 2016 | DDC 158.1--dc23
LC record available at https://lccn.loc.gov/2016046961

Published by
Loving Healing Press
5145 Pontiac Trail
Ann Arbor, MI 48105

www.LHPress.com
info@LHPress.com

Tollfree (USA/CAN) 888-761-6268
FAX 734-663-6861

Contents

Also by Diane Wing

Self-Help

The True Nature of Energy: Transforming Anxiety into Tranquility

The True Nature of Tarot: Your Path to Personal Empowerment

Fiction

Trips to the Edge: Tales of the Unexpected

Thorne Manor... and other Bizarre Tales

Coven: The Scrolls of the Four Winds

In loving memory of my baby brother, Steven

Part I: The Happiness Perspective

Is happiness possible?

Everybody wants a happy life, but it is elusive to many.

I recently spoke to a woman about the idea of happiness. She stated that she felt being truly happy is not possible, that you can be happy in a certain circumstance, such as getting a promotion or receiving a gift, but not happy in general. How sad to feel as though no one can be truly happy. I disagree with this point of view. I know people who are incredibly happy with their lives, including me. It has nothing to do with how much money they have. In fact, those I know with the most money are the least happy overall.

The ones who have true happiness are the ones who feel a sense of fulfillment. They live a life that is perfect for who they are at their core, living in accordance with their true nature. They develop a lifestyle that includes self-control and taking responsibility for what they create in their lives. They revel in the small daily joys that provide them with a laugh or a sense of discovery.

Those who live in fear of what may come next and who adopt a sense of helplessness and hopelessness are unhappy. The ones who continuously chase after a goal derived from what others say will make them happy find that joy is always just out of reach. Each individual must determine for him- or herself what it means to be happy. Define what happiness means to you and get aligned with it.

You likely have a wish list waiting to materialize. Is it a list of stuff or a way of being that you seek? What if all of your desires came true? Do you believe it is possible? Do you think you have the ability to bring good things into your life in a positive way?

Tough questions to be sure. You may fluctuate between self-trust and uncertainty. When doubt creeps in, it sets up the potential for self-sabotage and procrastination. Sabotaging the potential for your dreams to become reality allows you to remove responsibility for why you do not have the things you want. The truth is, we are responsible for manifesting every single thing that is in our lives.

Unfortunately, it seems so much easier to believe that you have absolutely no control over what is in your life, blaming it on fate or the things your relatives did to you. When you find yourself blaming others for what is going on in your world, take a step back and ask yourself how you are contributing to your success or difficulty. Go deep into your questioning and include your basic beliefs, the regular thoughts running through your mind, and your actions or lack thereof. A pattern will emerge that leads to the understanding of how you are the master of your life and what you are doing to bring things into being—positive or negative. You have brought everything into your life that exists there right now. Realizing this helps you to understand the immense power you possess to change whatever it is you no longer want and to manifest your desires.

What does your world look like right now? Is it bright with opportunities or dull with boredom? What do you want it to look like? Understand what each part of your life looks like until they all align. Depending on what is happening around you, your mood, your physical condition, and many other factors, your view of the world you live in can vary. In the sense that each of us has a reality based on our unique perception, everyone lives in a different world. This is the Law of Infinite Universes.

What goes on in your world? Do you have control, or do you feel helpless? Do you use your power, or do you submit to those around you? The decisions you make each day are based in the constructs and framework you have built, which are based on learning and experience and what you think is possible. Gauge where you are by conceptualizing what your world holds within it.

How Do You Want to Live?

We all have dreams of the perfect life, of a way of being on a daily basis that seems to elude the average person. Often, the idea of a different life is conceptualized by stepping out of the current circumstances into a whole new one. Generally, change happens gradually rather than all at once. The transitions that carry you toward your ideal life occur in small steps.

Thinking about the ideal life can be different from actually living it. It is worthwhile to test your ideas and experience them in small ways. Find ways to incorporate your ideal life into the life you live now. Gradually, that life will begin to manifest in bigger ways... or you may discover that this particular path is not something you really want. There may be certain things you need to let go of in order to live a certain way. It could mean that living more simply and freeing yourself from the aspects of your current life that hold you back may be necessary.

It takes courage to leave behind an old way of being. It takes the ability to go deep into yourself to discover a way of being that aligns with your true nature. It requires that you listen to yourself rather than the voices of those around you who tell you it cannot be done. Cultivate a strong vision of the ideal way of life and make the changes necessary to step into it fully.

Seeds Take Time to Grow

Growth requires time. When a seed is planted, the plant does not sprout up spontaneously. It needs time, nurturing, and nutrients to grow into its ultimate form in a healthy way. We live in a world that demands instant results, products that profess to give immediate cures or relief, programs that proclaim to change your life right away with little or no effort.

While it is true that there are moments when we have an epiphany and the resulting change seems instantaneous, it is more likely that the realization has built up over time and something you encountered in that moment triggered all the learning that led up to that point.

Are You Really Ready for a Change?

Have you found yourself saying, "I know things need to be different, but I do not know what to do to start making changes"? Or "I need a new direction," but you are not quite sure which path to go down, and then you place restrictions on how you approach the needed changes? The way you approach change determines the effectiveness of your efforts.

Some begin their search with a predetermined notion that is consistent with how things have always been. They search for the method or person that allows them to maintain their current view of themselves and their lives. When they hit upon something or someone that forces them to think differently, the approach is rejected.

Significant change requires nothing less than moving out of your comfort zone, challenging your beliefs, and the courage to make the necessary changes. If as you read that last sentence, you feel a tightness in your stomach and feel afraid at the thought of dumping all preconceptions about yourself and your life, then the question you really need to be asking is "Am I really ready to make the necessary changes that will bring me happiness?"

Here's the truth: making significant changes in your life is challenging, requiring commitment, honesty with yourself, and pushing yourself beyond your current thought process. When you are forced to consider a new perspective and have a big reaction to it—emotionally, physically, or mentally—it requires further examination.

In youth, changes happen faster and closer together. Progress is made with lots of small victories, and you learn about yourself along the way. As you approach forty years old, the tendency to stay in your comfort zone increases, and while the learning continues, the changes are fewer and farther between. Experiencing life-altering circumstances such as a death or divorce can move you forward or force you back, depending on your reaction to the situation. No matter what, these situations increase self-awareness.

With each piece of self-knowledge that is collected, you move up a notch in your development. Each shift puts you in a different mindset and brings you to a new level of understanding, ultimately requiring new strategies and a bigger push to get to the next level. The farther along you are on the path to self-awareness, the bigger the chasm between where you are and where you are trying to get. The time on the plateau creates complacency. It is easy to feel as though you have done the work and that you are where you should be, yet the Great Work of the self is never complete and affords you perpetual growth opportunities.

If you feel you have done the work and already know yourself, then monitor the questions you ask and the goals you set. Take note of when you look for the things that support your current view of yourself. Seek to move beyond where you have been. Read and listen to alternate perspectives, whether or not you agree with them, simply to expand your viewpoint. Change is imminent when you are uncomfortable and when nothing seems to work in your favor. Anxiety exponentially increases the closer you get to a major shift. When the transformation occurs, it is a relief, the weight is lifted, and you can see more clearly.

So are you ready to make a change?

The Pursuit of Happiness

Happiness is associated with meaning and purpose in one's life. There are numerous benefits of living a happy life. Think about times when you were depressed; often, they were followed by getting a cold. Now think about times when you had a period of happiness; you most likely did not become ill, but actually experienced a heightened sense of wellbeing and increased energy. When the world looks bright, there is excitement about what is around the next corner. To look forward to what the day brings enhances motivation and sense of purpose.

Those who suffer from depression and anxiety know the detrimental effects they have on one's life. Nothing seems worthwhile, life is riddled with fear about what may or may not happen, and the world looks gray. Happiness eliminates depression and anxiety. These states of being cannot occupy the same space at the same time. A sense of joy creates higher tolerance, more compassion, and attracts people who vibrate at that same happiness level. Gloom repels those of a higher vibrational level; a happy, positive disposition attracts those who strive for and have found joy in their own lives.

Shifting our focus from overcoming the negative to increasing the positive is a great way to cultivate happiness and tranquility. Tranquility is defined as an untroubled state, free from stress and filled with peace. It is up to us to choose the state we live in and to clear the blocks to a happy, peaceful life.

There are days when you are bombarded with external stressors and circumstances beyond your control that weigh on you and derail your attempts to live a serene life. While the circumstances may be unavoidable, your reaction to them is within your power to control. It is a conscious choice to succumb to the habitual response that has become automatic or to stop, breathe, feel your feet on the floor, and decide to react differently. If this is difficult to fathom, consider how many times getting upset helped the situation. In my experience, the answer is zero. It takes practice to shift from being upset to grounded and centered.

> **Exercise i-1:** Take the agitation and dump it into the ground (see chapter on grounding for ways to do this) and go into nature or your sacred space to recharge. To create a personal, peaceful place, choose a spot either inside or outside, smudge the area with your favorite herbs, beat your drum, call in whatever energies make you feel calm, and/or light a candle charged with the intention of setting tranquil energy in the space.

You Are Your Best Authority

One key to happiness is recognizing that you are your best authority. Listening to sources outside of yourself and giving external "experts" power over your decisions, your hope for the future, and your view of yourself is a recipe for misery. Some spiritual mentors, coaches, authors, and unethical practitioners of all sorts prey on those trying to overcome their challenges and who need help resolving even the most mundane issues.

To avoid handing over your power, ask questions, challenge the information, and even reject it completely if it feels right to do so. When receiving advice, check-in with yourself and see whether it feels right to you. If not, keep searching for the right person to guide you—one who embodies the principles that resonate with you. When you read a book that tells you to follow a specific way of being or to use a particular technique and it does not feel right to you, listen to yourself. Just because it is in writing does not mean it applies to everyone or that it is correct. I even encourage you to question what I am telling you now, in this book!

Use the four-part inner guidance system I discuss in my book *The True Nature of Energy: Transforming Anxiety into Tranquility*. When you hear a certain piece of information, how does it feel in your body? Do you tense up or relax? What thoughts go through your mind? Are they filled with fear and doubt or excitement and hope? How does it feel emotionally? Is there anxiety and depression, or do you light up? When you "ask" for Divine guidance on the information, do you get a green light or a red flag?

Maintain sovereignty always. Do not blindly trust; cultivate healthy skepticism. Do not assume you can trust everyone who says he or she is working in your best interest or who claims to be an authority. If someone says his way is the only way, that is a strong indicator to continue soul searching or even Google searching. Consider other opinions, especially your own. You are the best authority of what needs to happen in your life. You have power to make choices that are for your highest good. Embrace that power and learn how to cultivate your inner guidance. It is your best defense against charlatans and unethical practitioners, and it keeps the power where it belongs—with you.

Is Happiness a Matter of Luck?

Some people just seem lucky; no matter what they do, it all seems to work out for them. Others seem to walk around with the proverbial "black cloud" over their heads, drawing challenges, difficulties, and drama into their lives. What is the difference between these two types? What I have witnessed over and over is that those who are in a state of constant struggle expect to have problems and set-up limitations by finding all of the reasons things cannot happen. There is an inherent lack of trust that things will work out for the best. Those who are lucky tend to live in a state of gratitude, where they understand that they can take positive action toward their desires, yet do not feel the need to control how their wishes manifest. They have a generally accepting and optimistic attitude toward life, and those they surround themselves with tend to view life as an adventure, with problems that arise being opportunities to overcome and succeed. The more they open to possibilities, the more positive energies they attract. Essentially, they are creating their own luck and happiness—and you can too!

Back to Basics: The Need to Build a Strong Foundation

Some believe that happiness allows for an easy road, but it is quite the opposite. Living in joy requires focus, commitment, self-discipline, and self-knowledge. Before true happiness can be created, building a solid foundation is critical to successful work. The stronger you are mentally, physically, emotionally, and spiritually, the faster happiness enters your life.

Be healthy, mind, body, and spirit. Eat right, clear the clutter and clean your home, and strengthen your energy field with dumping, grounding, and protecting. A clear, fortified, and focused person is able to direct his or her life in a way that a scattered person cannot.

Your external environment says a lot about your internal state. Clutter and dirt in the home or in your sacred space reflects confusion, stuck energy, and a lack of self-worth. Trying to achieve the Happiness Perspective in this type of space produces muddled and ineffective results. Prepare the space by cleaning it while inserting the energies of gratitude, love, and reverence. Charge your cleaning solutions with the energy of protection and security. Hold the bottle of cleanser and send intentions that produce the type of environment you long for—peaceful, calm, safe, etc. Piles of clothes, papers, and other items serve to choke off the flow of energy. Clear the clutter to allow energy to flow freely through the space.

If you are feeling tense, upset, or ill, take steps to shift these energies and feel bright and purposeful. Take time to heal the malady. By doing so, your ability to manifest your desires exponentially increases. By approaching your daily routine in these ways, it translates into a more centered and focused way of being in which you are able to handle most situations in your life and direct your energy more effectively.

Everything Is Relative

Have you ever had something happen that upset you to no end and then you shared the situation with a friend who felt you were overreacting? You experienced the circumstance more intensely than your friend would have.

This is because everything is relative. If you had your hopes set on a particular goal, only to have everything fall through, it could be devastating. If, on the other hand, you saw the difficulties as a lesson and a stepping stone to an even better outcome, then it is likely to be motivating.

So the question becomes, in what context are you viewing the situation? Which beliefs are kicking in, and are they valid?

Let us stay with the idea of everything falling through. If you believe that there will never be another opportunity to fulfill your dreams, then it could result in depression. If you believe that the Universe is looking out for your highest good and things will work out for the best, the result is hope and understanding.

The idea of relativity is that everything has significance only in relation to something else. It is about context; nothing happens in and of itself; there is always a framework from which it is viewed and extended with internal or external circumstances applied. What one person feels is important may or may not be to someone else. It may crush one person and bring hope to another.

Putting things into perspective allows a heightened awareness of what the situation really holds. An extreme case is that of British physicist Stephen Hawking, a brilliant man who admits he was enjoying his social life a great deal and did not focus on his studies until he acquired the debilitating disease ALS at twenty-one. He was not expected to live past twenty-five, but he is now in his seventies. This would be devastating news under any circumstance, yet Stephen Hawking said that without ALS, he would not have accomplished even half of his groundbreaking work, let alone rise to hold Cambridge University's Lucasian Professorship of Mathematics, a position that has been held by only seventeen men, including the father of physics, Isaac Newton. Hawking said that the disease forced him to focus.

Now, think about how an initial bit of bad news turned out for the best. What were you able to accomplish that would not have been possible without that unexpected situation? It all depends on the context of the situation.

There are many ways to perceive objects, behaviors, and people. The circumstances within which they occur lead to particular interpretations. The definition we apply to the person or thing is influenced by its context. This then determines how we respond to it.

For example, a person is an attorney. The ability to make a good argument, to manipulate information, and to cite precedence is valued within the context of a courtroom. The attributes that make the person effective as an attorney are not welcome in personal disputes. I know several women married to attorneys who complain that their husbands tend to approach a marital argument in the same way they would in a trial. In their personal life, this behavior is defined as off-putting and unwelcome.

A man who spends every Saturday playing golf could be perceived by his significant other either to be taking time away from her or to be providing her with a welcome opportunity for some "me" time. This is determined by the context of her definition of what a relationship should be. If it is that as a couple you spend all of your free time together, then it will be viewed as negative behavior; if alone time is important, then it will be viewed as positive.

The interpretation of an astrological natal chart is influenced by the reader's perspective and the chart's focus. If the focus is on vocation, the chart data is interpreted in relation to the native's career opportunities and associated characteristics. If the reading focuses on health, the reader will interpret the same data in the context of medical astrology definitions. While the planetary positions are the same, their definitions change based on the context.

Start to notice how your personal definition of people and things is influenced by its context. How does your definition change based on the circumstances? Come up with your own examples. The main thing to note is that nothing is completely good or bad; rather it is initially neutral and its meaning and effect is dependent upon the context in which it is being perceived. Perception is reality, and so the way you see and define something determines your feelings, behaviors, and interpretations of it.

Say you need to traverse a quarter of a mile. If you are in good health, this is an easy task that is accomplished in minutes. If you have a problem walking, then it is a struggle to complete that short distance; it takes a lot longer, and results in frustration. How can the situation be dealt with to increase the joy in the experience?

If you insist on covering the distance without a cane, forcing yourself to push through without assistance, it is even harder. Add a cane and it becomes a bit easier but still frustrating and slow going. Add a walker and stability increases, along with confidence. Now, what if you added a scooter to the mix? The happiness quotient of traversing a quarter mile goes way up. It is easier, more enjoyable, and speeds up the process.

Exercise i-2: Here is something to ponder. Are you making things hard on yourself? Is pride, anger, or hopelessness the construct providing context to your situation?

Dealing with the symptoms (emotions) only puts a temporary patch on what is troubling you. Digging out the root is key to fully overcoming discomfort and entering into a happier view of the world. It increases your energy level, expands possibilities, and enhances understanding of what is in your life and how best to use the information held within the situation.

Exercise i-3: Pick a circumstance you are struggling with. Consider the emotions associated with that particular situation. What is the root of it? Is it anger at another person or at yourself? Is it that you have given up trying? Is it that you feel you can do it on your own without the right kind of help? Once the root is identified, list ways you can modify how you are viewing the situation and what types of assistance would be appropriate to move past it.

Look at everything within the context of the circumstances or the focus. What may seem negative in one context may be motivating in another. Everything is relative.

Part II:
Shift Your Perspective

Chapter 1: Regarding the Internal

Shift Your Perspective: On Adjusting

Whether at social or business events, I find that more and more people are taking stock of where they are now and the changes that need to be made for them to move forward in the most fulfilling way. Those who have awareness of the path they need to take often find it difficult to take the steps necessary to embrace fully the lives they envision for themselves. Those who are on the path of their true callings find it necessary to make constant changes and modify their approach to manifesting the lives they want.

The key to making changes of any kind is the willingness to adjust your thinking and your actions in accordance with what you want. Simply asking for it, praying for it, or envisioning it are not enough. You must take definitive action toward the vision. Remove any time-wasting activities that do not take you toward your ultimate destination. Reject relationships or circumstances that are unhealthy for you and that create energy drains.

No matter where you are on the path, maintain a dynamic mindset, for as you step from one level to another, pass through one cycle to another, adjustments need to be made. With each new experience, you gain understanding. This leads to an adjustment in the way you think about yourself and your future and creates new opportunities to fulfill your dreams. It may spark an idea you never could have had before or may allow you to see a path that was previously unavailable to you.

With each shift, with each new experience, your view of the world may change only slightly or may change in a profound way. In all cases, you are never the same as you were before, and so adjusting to the new way of thinking and being requires reconsidering your goals and modifying the actions you take. In this way, you align yourself with yourself and redirect your efforts to bring forth the new potential.

Stay cognizant of how experiences, relationships, and knowledge assist you in growing and allow the changes necessary to accommodate your new form. Use journaling, divination tools, and meditation to tap into the deeper meanings of your life. Seek out your reflection in those around you and gaze objectively at the results your energy creates in your life. See how your outer world begins to take the shape of your transition—you may change your home's decor, wear different clothing than you usually do, or purge items that no longer feel part of your heightened sense of self.

It is a marvelous thing when you see yourself growing and changing and taking the necessary steps to support that development, embracing that which is your true self, your true calling, and going forth in a centered, grounded manner that fosters additional awareness and understanding.

Exercise 1-1: Consider a recent shift in the way you think about yourself or your circumstances. How has this changed the actions you take? Have your priorities changed as a result? In what way? If you have not had a recent shift, think about a persistent way of looking at something and make a list of ways you can see it differently, whether you believe it right now or not. Look at it from several points of view other than the current one and choose one that feels right; then adjust to that new perspective accordingly.

Shift Your Perspective: On Anger

Think back to all the times you have been angry. Anger can result from a variety of reasons and takes on many forms. The energy of anger is directed at the perceived source—whether it is anger with the self, with someone else, or at a situation. It may be mixed with hate, disappointment, hurt, or aggravation. It may be justified... or not.

Some people feel that anger is a negative emotion to be avoided at all costs. Anger creates discordant energy that takes you off center. Loss of control in a fit of anger can prompt actions you may deeply regret later; whether it is something said or something done, the effects can be long lasting.

Anger as a primary view of the world, as in anger at others' behavior or at one's own circumstances, wears the person down and repels people from wanting to be around him or her. This type of person feels justified in his or her anger and holds on to it.

Blowing up out of anger can be exhausting and even dangerous, when it takes a violent form. Also, staying angry at a situation and talking about it over and over fuels the fire, intensifies the propensity to take regretful action, and keeps the negativity in place.

Sometimes, anger comes forward toward things that are out of a personal scope of control, such as death, war, the government, or the economy. The anger is attached to feeling helpless or powerless to change the situation. When that occurs, allow acceptance to replace anger and focus on uplifting aspects of life and ways to bring that higher vibration into the world.

Anger is more likely to appear when a person is fatigued, stressed, or upset. These lower the tolerance threshold and increase the likelihood that the response to certain triggers, like teasing, criticism, failure, etc., will result in lashing out in anger. To increase your tolerance, make sure you dump negativity and ground yourself on a regular basis. [See *Appendix* or

The True Nature of Energy: Transforming Anxiety into Tranquility by Diane Wing, M.A., on page 24.]

While these are valid reasons to look upon anger with disdain and to strive for self-control, there is a powerful use for anger. Anger, used to its best purpose, can be a catalyst for change. Any strong reaction is an indicator of a deep-seated belief or problem, and the forceful nature of anger is potent when channeled to make important changes.

Anger can come as the result of a social or personal injustice. This is a higher vibrational form of anger that can lead to the creation of social movements and personal actions that create positive change.

Anger that stems from feeling disrespected, undervalued, criticized, or unappreciated points to the need for personal change, including in the way the self is viewed or in the types of relationships engaged in.

Each person has a unique set of circumstances and triggers regarding anger. Anger can hold within it the seeds of change for the highest good. Be aware of how anger shows up, and tap into this powerful source of transformation.

Exercise 1-2: The following questions can help narrow the focus that will identify where you can direct this intense energy for the highest good:

1. Why am I angry? (Surface reason)

2. Why am I angry, really? (Underlying reason)

3. Am I truly angry, or is it really hurt, disappointment, or fear?

4. How does this situation make me feel about myself?

5. Is this a recurring situation/behavior?

6. Is this within my control to change?

7. What needs to change in order to reduce or eliminate recurring episodes of the situation/behavior?

8. How can I best use this energy to make significant changes in myself or the world?

Shift Your Perspective: On Anxiety

We all have bouts of anxiety. It can stem from internal or external sources. The potential for anxiety to arise is ever present. Some experience anxiety more frequently than others, self-perpetuating this state of being with negative self-talk and "what if" scenarios mentally played over and over. Some use it as a motivator to prepare for an important meeting or presentation.

Depending on the intensity of the anxiety, it can be debilitating or motivating. Anxiety can be self-managed in most cases, without the assistance of medication. With mindfulness toward your personal anxiety patterns, it is possible to become an anxiety expert able to control the level and intensity of the anxiety, as well as the duration.

Start by reviewing the list of causes below, and see which ones you find are most frequent in your anxiety repertoire.

Causes and cures of anxiety include:

1. **Cause:** Staying in limbo keeps the tension high.
   Cure: Make a decision! Even if you take another direction later, the act of making a choice relieves 80 percent of the stress.

2. **Cause:** Taking on the problems of others/trying to control others.
   Cure: Focus on what you need to do to take care of your own life and let others live their lives and make choices for themselves... even if you do not agree with them.

3. **Cause:** Trying to control circumstances that are out of your scope of influence.
   Cure: Recognize the aspects of the situation that you have direct control over and where you can make an impact. In every case, you have control over yourself, what you believe, the actions you take, and your emotional response to the situation.

4. **Cause:** Negative self-talk, such as "I'm not good enough," "Nothing ever works out for me," or "I have a dark cloud following me around."
   Cure: Be aware when the negative self-talk starts and stop it as soon as you can. Then challenge the thought with an alternative statement. Rather than "I'm not good enough," think of something you have done recently where you have succeeded—even a small accomplishment such as reorganizing your closet (which is no small task in some cases), and give yourself kudos for that.

5. **Cause:** Using global generalizations. Words like "all," "everything," "everyone," "nothing," "never," and "always" create a perspective that lumps together experiences rather than looking at them for their individual attributes.
   Cure: Take each situation separately and identify the strengths and challenges it presents.

6. **Cause:** Looking at the huge goal before you to the point of feeling overwhelmed and incapacitated.
   Cure: Cut the goal into manageable pieces and accomplish the ultimate goal one step at a time.

7. **Cause:** Having a doom and gloom perspective; believing the world is against you and that no amount of effort can change that. If you hear yourself complaining and being a naysayer to others, it not only prompts but exacerbates anxiety.

Cure: Find the silver lining; look for the glimmer of hope in an otherwise dark situation, seek to discover the lesson held within the difficult circumstance, and encourage others to achieve their goals.

8. **Cause: Resistance to change.**
   Cure: Be resilient in the face of change. Transitions and transformations are inevitable. Rather than fighting against the shift, see what benefit is held within it. Change can be a good thing.

9. **Cause: Stagnation.** This occurs when a shift or change is desired, but no action toward creating that change is taken.
   Cure: Do something you have never done before. Go to a new restaurant, visit an art museum, or attend a craft fair; get inspired to move beyond your comfort zone.

10. **Cause: Clutter and disorganization.** Too much stuff stifles the flow of energy through a space and causes mental confusion and agitation. Disorganization creates procrastination, which leads to anxiety.
    Cure: Purge your possessions. Clear the clutter. Physically clean your home/office/sacred space. You will feel lighter, as will the energy in the space, and you will be more focused and motivated.

11. **Cause:** Jealousy. This can include fear of abandonment or being left behind, a sense of not being good enough, and coveting others' experiences, accomplishments, and possessions.
    Cure: Appreciate what you have, identify your unique gifts, or identify what is lacking and take steps to attain it.

12. **Cause:** Fear, doubt, and worry stemming from personal perform-ance, meeting the expectations of others, health concerns for yourself or others, and uncertainty.
    Cure: Go outside and dump the fear, doubt, and worry into the ground. Let the earth take it and transform it. Now go ten feet from that spot and pull in fresh earth energy. Let it fill your body with brightness where you released the darkness. The issues may still be present, but being afraid of, doubtful toward, or worried about them will not help them go away or create a productive mindset. Dumping the heavy vibrations will give you increased energy with which to cope with whatever is going on.

The bottom line is that anxiety is inevitable. Your approach to managing it is critical to your mental, emotional, physical, and spiritual health. In most cases, you have the power to handle it and move on rather than maintaining the stress. For extreme cases such as phobias, post-traumatic stress disorder, or obsessive compulsive disorder, skilled professionals can help.

Becoming an expert in handling anxiety gives you more energy, greater resilience, and more happiness in your life.

> **Exercise 1-3:** To recognize your personal patterns of anxiety, ask yourself three questions: What triggers it? What sustains it? What allows you to release it?

Shift Your Perspective: On Change

Change can be stressful, especially big changes. When you feel like it is time to start getting on track and making changes in your life, it can feel daunting. Questions arise from your deepest fears. Will things feel too different? Am I doing the right thing? Do I have the strength and the ability to move forward with the necessary changes?

Cut yourself a break and realize that sweeping changes are not necessary in order to have a transformational experience. Even a minor change can create beneficial shifts that lead to even more positive results. For example, every time you catch yourself complaining about something, know that you are lowering your vibration and inhibiting your potential.

Replace the complaints with a resolution that addresses the problem. In this way, you will solve or eliminate the issue and your vibrational level will increase along with your self-confidence. You have control over the decisions you make, and making the decision to focus on the positive aspects of your life and adopting an attitude of gratitude will change your experience both internally and externally. The world looks much different when approached with optimism and positivity.

> **Exercise 1-4:** Choose one small thing that you want to change each month. As you succeed at each change, future changes will be easier to make. The size of the changes may increase, and you will be on the path to creating your destiny rather than being a victim.

Change must be initiated in order to see a difference in your life. I speak to countless folks who say they want their lives to be different, pause, and then say "but" and follow it with all the reasons why things will never change. And they are correct. They never will change as long as they believe it is not possible or that the obstacles before them are insurmountable.

The truth is that they have already decided to give up. That one decision is what needs to change. Deciding that the way things are right now is unacceptable is the first step in the process. Then it is time to envision your life the way you would like it to be. Forget the limitation and self-imposed restrictions. What do you want your life to look like? Do you want freedom? Do you want to work with a certain type of person or alone? Do you want to travel or stay home in your ideal environment?

Whatever it is, sit down and really take a look at your life, what you like and what you do not like about it, and then prioritize the changes you would like to make one at a time. Taking that first step is the most important, and the rest becomes easier after that.

So many folks struggle with change. They feel off-center, agitated, confused, and doubtful. The path they thought they were steadfastly traveling is shifting beneath their feet. Nothing feels the same, and there is uncertainty as to what to do.

You are in a time of major change; not only in the world, but also within yourself. You are being called to come fully into yourself, to do the work you were meant to do, and to get rid of the patterns that have kept you stuck. Those who choose to resist this time of shifting will experience the most anxiety. The harder one fights to maintain the current state of being, the denser the energies become, the rougher the road, and the deeper the stagnation.

Those who decide to be open to where their inner guidance and divine will takes them will experience discomfort, yet they will reach an unexpected new height. Life will take unanticipated turns, and this means changes in relationships, circumstances, and most of all, changes within the self. Allow these shifts to occur and revel in the release and joy to follow, while embracing the idea that everything has a natural cycle.

Natural cycles dictate the experiences you have. The ebb and flow of life brings change, some intense and some mild, all holding within it lessons and the opportunity for an internal shift. The more earth-shattering the change, the greater the moral it holds and the more significant the opportunity for growth.

> **Exercise 1-5:** Think back to the last major change that came about. Now list the top ten major life changes experienced since birth. What is the common thread throughout?

I did this exercise for myself and discovered that endings are the events that trigger an internal shift, a reassessment of life, and a significant learning experience. Graduations, the endings of relationships, and the deaths of loved ones bring about a contemplative time that contributes to my personal evolution. Each ending requires taking a different approach or way of thinking or behaving based on the lessons and life-altering changes that result from the experience. Nothing could ever be the same again.

The natural order of things creates cycles—seasons, moon phases, highs and lows in life experience and relationships—and calls you to flow with these rhythms in order to deepen your experience and your level of understanding. The energies of life, death, and rebirth are held within each day, month, and year. Each new day is the birth, noon brings the peak of the day's energy, and the sunset transitions us into night, holding the promise of another dawn.

The Wheel of Fortune card in tarot is symbolic of this inevitable rise and fall of energies and speaks to the need for adjusting both internally and externally to the new situation. It represents the expansion made possible through change and right action. Taking action is a necessary step in the process of change to avoid potential resistance. Pining for the way things used to be creates a standstill that could turn into stagnation.

Stay open to the possibilities of the cycle of change. Choose to address the circumstances first within the self and then bring it forward as an expression of new understanding and a fresh perspective. While it may not always seem so, remember that these natural shifts are not good nor bad, but necessary for personal growth and evolution. Everything happens for a reason and in its right (divinely dictated) time. Trust the process and the timing. It is for the highest good.

Shift Your Perspective: On Choices

Life is a series of choices. Choices create the future. Given this, from what perspective do you make choices? There are times when it seems that there is no choice, that there is only one way to proceed; yet there is always a choice; it is a matter of seeing the options.

Choices are restricted when all you see are obstacles. It is a self-limiting mindset that some take comfort in. If there are only obstacles, then there is no need to make a choice and take action; nothing can rectify the situation. That is when the sense of feeling stuck takes over. Feeling stuck can have the effect of habitual complacency, despite the outward complaining about the situation. Staying in this way of being is a choice. If this way of living is chosen, then accept it and know that there is comfort in it on some level.

If feeling stuck creates a sense of discomfort, then shift your focus to what is possible and then everything looks different. That is when options present themselves. Determine your intention and then generate options based on it.

Exercise 1-6: Your philosophical perspective will allow you to see options based on what you believe is possible. Go beyond that by removing perceived obstacles; that is, those obstacles that you anticipate, but that may not actually exist. Consider the situation as though no obstacles exist. Now what do you see?

The potential options should have exponentially increased. If they did not, check in with yourself and see how many of the options were eliminated because they seem out of your control. There may very well be some possibilities that are beyond your personal ability to manifest. In this case, take a different approach. Follow the intention or desired goal to the choice that takes you there with the least resistance and for your highest good.

If you still feel resistance, contemplate what is causing the anxiety or fear that creates reluctance to make a choice. The ultimate goal is to move beyond the current circumstances, so even if it is a minor shift, it is a start. Many times, larger goals require smaller steps to get there. Look at the issue in smaller bits and then generate options for each one.

By seeing the situation objectively and in bite-sized pieces, the first step will be easier to take and not so anxiety provoking. Gradual change will occur using this approach. Allow yourself to make choices based on the small sub-issues that make up the whole. Visualize the possibilities if just this one small piece of the puzzle is addressed. Once a choice has been made regarding that piece, go on to the next.

Keep in mind that the only thing stopping you from making a choice that changes your circumstances and from creating your ideal future is you. The idea that others are stopping you is a rationalization that keeps you in the circumstances with which you have grown familiar and comfortable. You are choosing to submit to the advice or opinions of your parents, friends, employer, spiritual leader, or significant other. And if you choose to maintain the status quo, accept full responsibility for that and find joy within it.

The opportunity to make choices is available each and every day. If you do not feel ready to change your approach today, then there is always tomorrow. But if you yearn for a new path, to feel inspired, to wake up each day looking forward to expressing yourself in the world, then do not wait too long, for each time you delay choosing the path that takes you closer to who you are and what you want your life to represent, the harder it is to free yourself from the trap of complacency as you watch your life go by. Ultimately, it is never too late, and it is always your choice.

Shift Your Perspective: On Desire

Do you complain that you are not getting what you want out of life or that nothing positive happens for you? When asked what steps you have taken toward your goals, the response is "Nothing yet, but I'll get around to it." This is extremely common, enough to justify the commercial manufacture of a round medallion imprinted with the word "TUIT" on it. Picture yourself receiving this round TUIT. Now that you have one, it is time to apply some self-discipline to the process.

You know you have the skills, the intelligence, and the desire to reach your goals. Now it is time to take disciplined action. Wake up and decide that today is the day you will apply willpower toward your desire.

Manifestation requires deliberate action, decision making, and resilience. To persist despite delays or missteps is to stay disciplined and focused on what you are trying to create in your life. Use self-control to avoid behaviors that will take you off the path and to maintain personal will to stick with positive choices.

> **Exercise 1-7:** Hold yourself accountable or find someone else who will, and vow to take small steps each day, accomplishing the next task that moves you closer to what you want.

What do you seek? You say it varies depending on the aspect of your life you focus on—work, relationship, home, personal development. Yet if you take all of the facets of your life and examine what you are striving toward, there is probably an overarching desire that you can identify as your *quest*.

It may be that you seek love and security in your life—this would encompass having healthy relationships, a solid source of income, and a safe place to live. If you seek self-expression and personal development, this again spans all aspects of life.

As you identify your quest, know that it is what drives your behaviors, beliefs, and impacts every aspect of your life.

Intention directs energy toward manifesting a particular desire. If the desire is to hold on to a relationship, idea, behavior, way of being, or situation that is coming to its natural end, caution is needed. There is a natural cycle of death in all things so that new energy can enter. Seeking to prevent the natural process of release hinders your growth and prohibits the beginning of what is trying to be born. Your energy is best used to smooth the transition from death into birth, knowing that with each shift and change, your power grows, enabling your desires to materialize.

Shift Your Perspective: On Discomfort

Are you comfortable in your discomfort? Have you found it easier to maintain your life in a way that perpetuates the need to complain, yet you do nothing significant to address it?

Discomfort comes in many forms: physical, emotional, mental, and spiritual. The resulting pain is there to bring your attention to something that is not serving you and that requires closer inspection. Everything is connected; physical pain is exacerbated by mental, emotional, and spiritual distress. For example, depression and anxiety can intensify or present as physical pain, while physical pain can bring about depression and anxiety.

To clear the discomfort, the root cause must be addressed. It will persist until you spend some time considering the source. It may simply be a physical issue that only a doctor can treat; at the same time, there are underlying metaphysical associations for most illnesses. Once the spiritual, mental, or emotional issue is resolved, the physical pain subsides.

Exercise 1-8: Alleviating the pain is most effective using a multi-level approach. Choose a discomfort or pain you are currently experiencing. For the purpose of example, let us say you are having heart palpitations and shortness of breath. The first level of treatment is physical, getting a check-up to ensure there is no actual heart anomaly. Once that is eliminated, consider when these symptoms occur. Is it emotional, primarily taking place during times of intense stress? Could it be an anxiety response to an external or internal trigger? Now move to your mental layer. Are your thoughts prompting the anxiety? Does fear, doubt, and worry creep in and trigger the anxiety? Now on the spiritual plane, do you believe you are alone with your troubles or that you can release this pain, trusting that the Universe is there to support you?

Simply addressing one aspect without consideration of the other three will perpetuate the discomfort and promote a sense that you are trying "everything," but nothing is working. In this case, you may be trying every medical intervention available, but you are doing nothing to support and explore the other three layers of existence. The same goes for focusing only on the spiritual part and none of the others. Finding the root cause and making necessary changes to resolve it will create simultaneous changes on every level.

Additionally, centering on your overall vibrational level instead of one particular behavior gives you the power to change simultaneously all aspects of your life that need improving. The nature of the energy in your life either drives you toward positive activities that result in being motivated, inspired, and creative (high vibration), or it moves you toward behaviors that diminish your energy such as smoking, overeating, or experiencing lack (low vibration). Changing the energies within and around you provides the power to change any condition in your life. By raising your overall vibration, you minimize or obliterate the lower vibrations.

Discomfort may arise as you seek to make changes in your life. Notice which part of the transition is causing you to resist. The distress is part of the lesson inherent in the effort to change. Coming into yourself and, ultimately, into your power is no easy task; there will be discomfort along the way. Persisting despite the discomfort helps develop willpower through controlling those negative thoughts. The will determines your next move, choice, and thought. It is your ability to control your emotions and impulses. It is what allows you to achieve self-control and self-discipline.

Discomfort is an indicator that something needs to change. Some choose to live with it, get used to it, and give up trying to change it. On some level, it is just not worth the effort it requires to surmount it. It is easier to keep functioning in the same patterns and deepening the thoughts, behaviors, and beliefs that triggered it to begin with. There is a comfort that turns to a habitual way of being. There is a deliberate choice being made to embrace this lifestyle.

That said, the other choice is to use that same discomfort to identify the things in your life that need to shift in order to live the life you truly want. Decide you want things to be different and that you are tired of living with discomfort; then take appropriate steps to get on track.

Shift Your Perspective: On Doubt

Doubt. No matter how confident you are, there are times when doubt comes at you full force. It may sneak up on you one situation at a time, or it could hit you full force after one incident that takes you from absolute certainty to complete uncertainty. You look for external validation that what you are feeling is valid; someone to tell you that you are overreacting. But no one is available right now. So you wallow in doubt, which turns to worry, which turns into anxiety.

We all know that self-doubt is detrimental; that is, when you do not trust your inner guidance or when you do not trust your potential. Yet there are times when doubt is a good thing, such as doubt about a particular action you are getting ready to take. It gives you the pause that gives the chance to confirm your decision.

When acting hastily, new doors will not be opened. Sometimes, a little doubt can prevent you from making a mistake. This type of doubt gives you the opportunity to learn more about the direction you are contemplating, to cultivate additional needed skills before proceeding, and to go into an objective self-assessing mode to see the situation more clearly.

When something is brought to your attention that makes you rethink what you are doing or what you want, pay attention to see whether it is something that helps you adjust the way you are approaching what you are doing or the way you are looking at the situation. This can be helpful in considering whether to move forward with certain relationships / partnerships or assessing whether or not you are ready to do certain work or to take on particular challenges.

I met a woman named Sarah, who had just worked her way through a crisis of faith. She had worked for over twenty years as an executive for a large corporation. When she was laid off, rather than look for work at another company, she decided to pursue her dream of owning her own business. She worked tirelessly at learning how to build a strong foundation for her business. She networked and built her client base. She loved what she was doing and had high hopes for success. Sarah was a confident woman who generally achieved whatever she set her mind to do.

After two years of continuous effort, she was further along, but still not making the money she had been making as an employee of a company. The summer lull in activity chipped away at her hopes of hitting a six-figure salary that year. Logically, she knew that it takes about five years before a business starts making any money. Emotionally, she was disappointed that her efforts were not producing the revenue she anticipated.

That night, an email came through with an opportunity that perfectly suited her. It was for an international company that was a forty-five-minute commute. Sarah was fully qualified and knew one or two people at the organization that had posted the position. Her mind calculated what she could earn if she got the job, how she could stop running on the marketing wheel, and get that regular paycheck she was so used to receiving. Doubt about the wisdom of trying to accomplish her dream goal in a difficult market crept in. She could stop worrying about trying to get that next client or fill the next group program. She seriously began to consider applying for the position.

Sarah's body tensed and the worry increased as she tried to picture herself in an office environment. She could do it, but did she really want to? After such a long period being on her own, would she be able to tolerate the office politics and having to focus on someone else's vision? Did she want to put on a suit and become corporate again? Fear blew in like a cloud across her mind.

What if she gave up now when her business was on the verge of really taking off? What about all of the things that were in the works that were pending and needed a bit of nurturing to come to fruition? What if this were the last opportunity she'd have to make her dream come true? It would be giving up on what she knew she was meant to do to take the safe route. She had heard many stories of entrepreneurs who gave up right before their big breaks came. She began to clench her teeth.

As she envisioned herself back at a regular job, in an office, commuting each day in rush-hour traffic, wearing uncomfortable clothing, she knew it did not feel right. She had done it for years and learned what she needed to go out on her own. Sarah was not one simply to give up. Every cell in her body was rejecting the vision of working for someone else. Her inner guidance was refusing to let her be comfortable with this idea.

Her logical mind kicked in. She was not struggling financially. She had clients who depended on her. She loved what she was doing. She had the self-discipline and focus to make this a successful venture. She realized that what sparked the doubt was the quiet period that she recognized as seasonal. Her spreadsheet showed that she was ahead of the prior year in earnings. Sarah realized the downtime was necessary for her to regroup, rejuvenate, and work on marketing plans and other solitary work that was difficult to address when there was a rush of clients.

Sarah decided to rededicate herself to her business, to renew her sense of purpose, to reignite her passion, and to refocus her energies on what she had been putting on the back burner. Her body relaxed, her mind was clear, she smiled, and her inner guidance smiled back at her. At that moment, she knew her path was the right one. This bout of doubt was necessary to get her back on track and recommitted to her vision. She was grateful for this time of questioning herself and her goals and for the resulting clarity.

Later that day, she spoke to a trusted friend who affirmed everything she had considered. It was good to have a reality check to make sure she was not completely off base. It validated what her intuition already knew. She resolved to learn to trust her instincts more.

The entire episode lasted about sixteen hours. She did not allow her pondering to lead her down the road to full-blown anxiety. A bit of fear had crept in, but she realized that she needed to address her lapse in confidence and reestablish her reasons for wanting to achieve this goal in the first place. Her energy was beaming, and she was ready to get back to work. That afternoon, she completed five tasks that had been put off for way too long, and she felt like she was back on track.

How long will you stay in doubt mode? You ride the wave hoping something will come along to shake you out of it. The doubt makes you uncomfortable; the worry serves to bring forward your deepest fears. The longer you stay in this zone, the greater the anxiety becomes.

Exercise 1-9: Next time you feel doubtful—about your direction, your actions, your beliefs, or whatever—allow some time to uncover what the core issue is. Then lessen the length of time you feel doubt by facing head-on the very things causing you to feel this way in the first place.

The truth is that doubt serves a purpose. It allows you to proceed with caution, and it keeps you on your toes. Healthy skepticism is important, but not when it becomes debilitating. Do not question yourself into a corner. The doubt zone is where you can do some deep soul searching and uncover the things that will keep bubbling up until they are fully addressed.

Patience with yourself can be harder than having patience with others. Self-care during this time is crucial in order to push through the challenge and get to the other side. Withdraw and allow yourself some time alone. Doubt gives you a waiting period before making any major decision. The reward is at the other side, in the form of feeling safe, comfortable, and certain about your conclusion.

Shift Your Perspective: On Fear

Fear is debilitating. And even more frightening is the number of times we create a self-imposed prison of fear. The scariest trap is the self-created one. Fueled by anxiety and the "what if" self-talk, the reinforced concrete blocks that imprison us are built from the constant negative internal chatter. We build a wall of inactivity made of fear, doubt, and worry, where limbo is the punishment, keeping us stuck in the same old patterns.

We cycle through periods of fear and confidence, a natural rhythm that is a combination of feeling physically, mentally, emotionally, and spiritually capable, plus a string of positive external events. The key is to have confidence and a positive outlook during the most challenging times.

What we forget is that we have the power to break down the walls of fear. Strength is within each of us. It bolsters the spirit and allows forward progress. It can be developed in a way that maintains momentum regardless of what is going on around us. This is the nature and the benefit of fostering self-confidence.

We have the ability to shift our thinking, our perspective, and our focus. The more we take control of our thoughts and emotions, the more likely we are to stay strong during the most difficult situations. While there will be times when it feels more challenging to practice this type of self-control, the more habitual it becomes when things are well, the more likely it is to navigate through stressful times successfully.

Cultivating self-confidence is crucial to our overall wellbeing. Trusting our abilities, formulating a clear intention, and creating a calm resonance within is the essence of confidence. Knowing ourselves is essential to understanding the natural gifts we have and the way we view the world. Perspective affects our view of ourselves and the world around us, and there are times when a shift in perspective is needed to clear the way for forward movement.

The more confidence we have, the more willing we are to change perspective without fear. There is no need to hold on to outmoded ways of thinking and being that only serve to drain our vitality.

Exercise 1-10: If you are ready to clear the path toward inner strength and confidence, start with this:

1. Releasing fear starts with understanding what we are afraid of. What triggered the fear to begin with? Once we determine that, then identify the behavior that results from that fear. Track when the fear is most likely to well up, and look at the situation objectively. Breathe deeply and relax your body. Envision the situation working out for the best.

2. Ask yourself what you are really afraid of. Go down as many layers as needed to get to the core of what is prohibiting your progress. For example, "I'm afraid of losing [a particular person] from my life." Next layer, "If I lose that person, then I'm afraid that I will have no support." Next layer, "If I have no support, then I'm afraid I won't be able to live a happy life." Next layer, "If I can't live a happy life, then I'm afraid I'll be alone and miserable," etc.

3. Ask yourself what will happen if you change the thoughts and feelings you have held on to for so long. How will your life change for the better? How will it change in ways that create fear? For example, "If [a particular person] is no longer in my life, then my opportunities to experience new relationships opens up."

4.   To overcome fear, you need to feel safe. What makes you feel vulnerable?

5.   Change one small thing in your life and note what happens. For example, say no to something you do not really want to do, but would have said yes to from fear of disappointing someone or being afraid of disapproval.

6.   Journal about the fear and the mindset that keeps you stuck.

We can bring peace into our life by releasing fear. Fear is a result of both past experience and anxiety about potential threats that may or may not transpire. When we are afraid, it affects behavior, health, and our ability to have loving relationships.

Fear may manifest as the need to control situations and people in order to feel safe, as paralysis and the inability to take action to keep us comfortable in our discomfort, or even as lashing out to intimidate those around us into doing or not doing what we want. These behaviors tend to push people away and prevent us from achieving our goals.

We all have moments of difficulty and weakness, yet we are capable of rallying by building our confidence and trusting in our ability to make positive changes and create our ideal future.

Shift Your Perspective: On Finding Yourself

Thousands, if not millions, of people are searching for a better life, meaningful work, happiness, and a sense of inner peace. They are tired of just getting through the day and want something more. What they have tried is not working; they are frustrated at not knowing how to get out of the rut and start on their true path.

It is true that in living your purpose, the world is a brighter place, there is boundless energy, and a looking forward to what the day brings. But so many experience the exact opposite: a dull existence, their energy drained, and nothing to look forward to. Why would anyone stay in that state of being? There are many reasons—one of the biggest being uncertainty of how to move forward, what steps to take, and where to begin.

The good news is that it is never too late to begin your search, to get on your true path, to do the work you were meant to do in this lifetime, and to experience life in a way that brings contentment and joy. There are so many ways to begin; it is just a matter of choosing the one you are most comfortable with. Start slowly and get acclimated to opening to the shift that will change your life forever.

One thing that prevents people from taking the first step is knowing that their lives will never be the same. That is a bit scary and makes all kinds of fears bubble up, like how it will change their current relationships, jobs, and self-images.

Exercise 1-11: Test the waters with a journal entry about what your life would look like if you were engaged in your dream vocation. Even if you do not know what that is just yet, dream a little without boundaries and write as if you are living the dream. What does your life look like? Who is there with you? Where do you live? How do you feel?

Once you "try on" your new situation, mindset, or vocation, it takes away the unknown and puts you squarely in a state of desire to be living the life you really want. For help in determining your ideal vocation, engage a friend who knows you well to brainstorm about what you are good at, or connect with a professional coach who can really get you on the fast track to getting your life in gear.

I remember when I was uncertain of what I was meant to do in this lifetime. The crazy thing was that I really knew where my passions were at a very young age, but I was steered away from them by well-meaning adults who insisted that I would never be able to support myself if I did not pursue a traditional vocation (physician, attorney, accountant, etc.). Taken on a detour that actually enhanced my ability to pursue my dream goals, I attempted many courses of study and accepted jobs that paid well, but they only got me so far in the realm of personal satisfaction. One thing that remained consistent was my love of reading and writing about personal development, metaphysics, and the unique phenomenological journey each of us travels. My deep study of a wide range of philosophies, psychological approaches and theories, and spiritual concepts brought me to understand that it all amounts to coming fully into yourself by way of profound self-awareness.

Finally coming full circle and allowing myself to do the work I love, each day is bright and fulfilling. My vocation is my vacation, for I would rather be doing this work than living a life of leisure. There is a constant stream of ideas and boundless energy to bring them into being. My work helps others to achieve their ultimate dreams and goals, and, truly, there is nothing better than that. I love seeing people come fully into themselves, especially when they thought it was a dream that could never become reality.

If your days do not feel like this, I strongly encourage you to take stock in how you are living your life. Ask yourself whether there is a better way, a better direction, a path that is powerfully aligned with your true nature and what you want your life to become. It is never too late to change your course! If the thought of opening this line of thinking seems overwhelming, there is no need to walk the path alone. Consult with those who have your best interest at heart or even a professional, keeping in mind that at some point, the path you walk is solely yours to decide.

Shift Your Perspective: On Mindfulness

Have you ever found yourself doing something out of sheer habit? It has become second nature and you do not even realize you are doing it. It can be an action, a behavior, a way of thinking, or a reaction to certain interactions. They are the automatic things you do that require no thought, as with writing your signature, or that we choose not to give thought to, such as the way we respond to others.

Whenever we have a reaction to something, it is generally based in an underlying belief that has been present for such a long time that we no longer pay attention to it and assume that it is true. For example, giving up when things get hard, due to the underlying belief that it will not work out anyway, or automatically taking control of a situation because of the belief that it will not get done properly unless you do it yourself. In most cases, there is no conscious thought given to why you are giving up or why you feel the need to do everything yourself; you just do it.

When mindfulness enters the picture, it allows a deeper understanding of your motives and your beliefs. Let us go back to giving up in challenging circumstances. You have just thrown in the towel. Now ask yourself why. Was it too exhausting? Did you feel like you were not making progress? Did you decide you were going down the wrong path? Understanding the rationale behind the behavior gives you the opportunity to use the information when assessing future scenarios. It may not really be that nothing ever works out the way you planned; the reality may be that the choices you make as to where to put your energy need to be addressed.

Now for the example of needing to do everything yourself. When you catch yourself doing it, stop and think. Is it because you believe others are incapable? Is it because you prefer to be in control? Do you like the idea that everyone depends on you? Do you like to hear others admire your efforts? Or is it really that you are the only one who can accomplish certain tasks? Dig down deep to discover the true reason you feel you must do everything yourself. Now assess your energy level and your available time. Would it be more efficient to delegate certain tasks so you would have more time to do the things only you can do? Those would be the things that require your unique stamp.

Exercise 1-12: Start paying attention to what you do, how you react, and how you feel as often as possible. Be mindful about your motives, thoughts, and behaviors. You will find that this awareness helps you know yourself better and enables you to make necessary, permanent changes that lead to living the life you want.

Shift Your Perspective: On Motivation

Each day you wake up with a new opportunity before you... to do something never before attempted, to complete a project, to excel at work, to make a difference in someone's life. Whether or not that opportunity is grasped depends on what motivates you, what drives you to attain that goal.

What motivates you? Everyone is unique when it comes to motivation. You may be driven by money, love, fame, or the desire to be taken care of by others. There is no right or wrong motivation, no judgment in what motivates one person over another; it is just a statement of fact.

The importance of understanding the rationale behind your actions and decisions is that it colors your choices and your direction. Once identified, you will find that what motivates you in one area of your life runs through all aspects. Move past the surface of what you think motivates you.

For example, if you look at your life and say that money is what motivates you to get out of bed in the morning, then look more closely at what that money is providing—security for you and your family, the ability to live a certain way and buy certain things, or even the freedom to pursue creative interests.

If love is the motivator, go deeper. What about love provides you with the reward you seek? Is it validation that motivates you? Acceptance? Companionship?

If you say that nothing motivates you, ask yourself whether you have the desire to feel motivated and inspired. Are others telling you that it is important to be motivated toward a goal of some sort? It may be that your goal is to watch as much TV as possible. And that is okay. Just recognize that your motivation for your choices may be that you prefer to disconnect from the outside world or that watching TV gives you the most peace. In that sense, peace and relaxation is what motivates you.

Exercise 1-13: To feel motivated and inspired, ask yourself what it is you are seeking in your life. How do you want your life to look? What kinds of people would you like to interact with and why? What makes you feel good and why?

Whenever there is difficulty in feeling motivated, it is because nothing can be identified that would be worth making significant changes for. Getting to the core of what is important to you will reveal the deep sense of reward that is the motivating factor for your life.

Now consider your motivation for the way you treat people. Is it out of jealousy, low self-esteem, control, or fear? Or do you act as a result of a desire for others to do well and manifest what they want in life? Are you kind and supportive because you seek approval, or is it because you are called to do so out of true concern for others? Determining the motivating force underlying action allows you to understand why you make the choices you do.

Let us take the example of acting out of control. You may feel you are doing whatever it is for someone's "own good," but the bottom line is that you are saying that person is not capable of taking control of his own life or making his own decisions. And at times, this may be true; however, the person must have the opportunity to learn for himself, especially if he has not requested your assistance.

The challenges placed in his path are to help him learn and grow. To remove that obstacle for someone without his consent is to step into his karmic path and deny him the opportunity to strengthen himself and learn from his experience.

In this context, "Do unto others as they would have you do unto them," feels more appropriate than "Do unto others as you would have them do unto you." Not everyone wants to be treated the same as you do; it is important to recognize what the other person wants and not to insert into his life something you think he should have or what you would want for yourself.

Recognize that what is best for someone may not be what you think is right, and understand your motivation for the ways you interact with others. This kind of awareness will change the way you look at the world and create a lighter, more harmonious way of being.

Shift Your Perspective: On Negativity

These days, it is so easy to fall under the spell of the media and the naysayers. The more we watch, the more likely it is to adopt the negative thoughts and feelings of the news and people who have a pessimistic view of the world. We all know them: people who believe they have a dark cloud following them around and that the end of the world is near. Well, they are correct, for they brought the storm upon themselves and have set about building the bomb shelter, whether physically, mentally, emotionally, or spiritually, to await ultimate destruction.

Here's how it works: Whatever you focus on, whatever your feelings are put toward, is what will ultimately manifest in your life. Your actions follow the thoughts that create the vision. Dwelling on disease, financial difficulties, or a sense of lack in general serves to bring expression to it in your life. Controlling the feelings you focus on is important; imagine embracing only the thoughts and feelings that contribute to your happiness!

It is all a function of the conscious mind impressing itself upon the subconscious mind. The subconscious creates your reality and brings it into the physical world. Be careful what you think and feel. To express the notion that I *will be healthy* implies that you are in a state of lack or illness. Saying instead I *am healthy* puts you into a state of mind that what you want is already in your life. Support yourself by addressing emotional disturbances in healthy ways, and do not focus on feelings of regret or failure, for they serve to bring physical disruptions along with emotional.

Exercise 1-14: Notice when a negative thought comes to mind. Shift it to a positive statement that calls into question the validity of the negative one. For example, change "My efforts will never amount to anything" to "I enjoy the process of bringing about my vision" or even "I am learning new skills along the way." In this manner, the focus is on the joy found in the moment. After all, the path may shift along the way, and the new perspective fosters flexibility and continued happiness wherever the road ultimately leads.

Be positive, be happy, and behave as though your desires have already been fulfilled. Watch your world change into the wonderful place you always knew it could be...the wonderful place you know it is!

Shift Your Perspective: On Self-Trust

Do you trust yourself? Or do you ask everyone else what you should do? Self-trust is an essential component of happiness. The idea that others know better what is best for you is what keeps you stuck and in a state of powerlessness.

Fretting over making a mistake maintains a state of limbo, which in turn fuels anxiety. Take a chance and make a choice. If you require guidance, ask the Universe to help you open to the direction that is for your highest good. Whatever you choose will be what you need to do in that moment. Do you believe you would not intentionally make a decision that causes yourself harm? If you feel you need more information before making a choice, then gather what is needed, but ultimately, reserve sovereignty over your right to decide your life.

Each day, there are many opportunities to acquire information from a variety of sources—friends, the Internet, books, teachers—yet too infrequently is most trustworthy and always available source of information consulted: your own internal guidance. It is the most powerful source of counsel, and the most difficult to trust.

You walk through the day putting more faith in others' opinions and thoughts before your own. As a child, you grow up being told that your parents or authority figures know better, and that you need to defer to their guidance. Fear of being judged or criticized for doing the wrong thing also enters into the equation. This creates a barrier when trying to develop your intuition; self-trust is required for listening to the guidance that comes through.

Without self-trust, the world seems uncertain, decisions feel arduous, and you give away your power to others who may or may not have your best interest at heart. Disappointment with the outcomes resulting from the advice of others creates a sense of distrust and causes self-admonishment for listening to them in the first place—and the cycle of self-deprecating talk begins, eroding your self-trust even more.

The quest for self-trust often starts with discovering that someone you trusted either deceived you in his or her ability to help or motivation for doing so. It turns out that the person is not the authority he or she claimed to be or had a self-serving motive for guiding you in a certain way. You realize that you have given away your power and are doing things that others want you to do rather than taking action toward what you want for yourself. It triggers the dilemma of trusting the guidance of others or finally realizing that inner guidance is the most reliable source for decision making and determining your path in life.

At this point, it is time to face the fear of criticism and judgment if you make a mistake. The fear may be so intense that you refuse to answer the call for change and commit to the journey. To address these fears, a mentor is needed, one who is cheering you on and who focuses on your highest good. This person can be a friend, a book on the subject, or a professional. The key here is to have someone who serves to guide you toward independence, who helps you overcome the fear of the journey before you, and who helps you practice trusting your own guidance.

Engaging a mentor may feel counterintuitive to the idea of independent thinking; however, the mentor's role is to focus on alleviating the fear so the journey can begin in earnest. The mentor serves as a safe place to practice trying out the new behavior of self-trust and to be held accountable for the results of your decisions. The mentor prepares you to face the unknown, yet a mentor can only go so far with you; eventually, you must face the unknown alone. Through the mentor's encouragement, you begin to trust yourself to travel your unique path and to walk toward your future with calm certainty.

The real journey begins when you cross the first threshold of change, when you have decided to take responsibility for whatever happens, come what may. You agree to face the consequences and take on the challenges of trusting yourself.

As this leg of the journey unfolds, you are tested by the Guardians of the Threshold who block the way as they seek to keep you uncertain and raising doubt that you have the ability to succeed without them. They want to keep things as they are. Phrases such as, "What do you want to do that for?" or "I have seen others fail by making that choice," put the seed of doubt into your mind and water it to grow out of proportion. They are the naysayers, the complainers, and the controllers who hide behind a wall of "for your own good," when what they want and what you want are not the same things. They test your resolve and attempt to talk you out of moving forward. Battling against that self-doubt requires consistent challenging of that internal voice that says you cannot do it.

Enemies are around every corner, waiting to take you off center, and the big three are fear, doubt, and worry. They erode confidence. The better prepared you are to overcome these, the faster you can move past the first hurdle. This includes the use of allies, who support your quest for independence and self-trust. These are the friends and mentors who help you think through problems on your terms with questions such as, "So what do you plan to do about that?" or "What do you think the best approach would be?" These inquiries may also be posed to yourself to combat the negative internal voice that calls your resolve into question.

Moving past the Guardians of the Threshold and the internal and external enemies, you approach the most dangerous leg of the journey and enter the cave of darkness wherein lies the desire of your quest. It is the place where it is time to face the fear, take a risk, and make a decision on your own. It is a proving ground for you to gain experience and to validate that you are capable of trusting your own judgment.

Choose something small at first, something that prevents forward motion, but does not have severe consequences. Remember, you are building up confidence and self-trust; you do not have to jump across the chasm to see whether you can make it without a bridge. Understand that this could result in a mistake where judgment from yourself or others occurs. The ordeal asks you, "Will you move past it and are you willing to try again?" Surviving choices that create unintended outcomes teach that mistakes are not the end of the world, but rather an opportunity to change course or to gain knowledge.

With each choice comes the opportunity to gain a positive outcome, and with each upswing comes the ability to choose wisely and to trust the decisions that move you forward on the path. With persistence, you develop resilience, and the grand reward of self-trust awaits.

Exercise 1-15: Check in with how you are feeling in the moment before taking action. Does the choice you are about to make cause your body to feel calm or agitated? Are you making a decision during a time of high anxiety or out of depression or fear? Dump the negativity and ground yourself to get centered, and then make the appropriate choice. Doing so will help you develop self-trust and reduce the need to depend on others' opinions.

There may be times when you have setbacks, when, despite success, you are still pursued by the enemy of self-doubt, but on the quest for self-trust, it is all about learning what you are capable of. Self-trust is the first step toward achieving self-confidence. When you trust yourself, it means that you put faith in your own decisions and opinions, while staying grounded and centered. When you identify what you seek, consider your options, and choose wisely, you stay on the path of building self-trust, a place within yourself that is unshakeable and assured.

Inner Magick—A term used to refer to the intuitive abilities and unique gifts that everyone possesses. It differs from magic with a "c" in that "magic" refers to the realm of the illusionist. You are the Magician, orchestrating and creating your life in accordance with your true self. This cannot happen if you give away your power. The power that comes from within starts with self-knowledge and is reinforced through self-confidence. Developing self-control and focus are two ways to enhance your ability to create. Believing in yourself is critical when it comes to manifesting your desires. Strengthen your imagination and ability to envision the ultimate result. Setting your mind and focus to something and seeing it clearly while believing it is possible allows you to bring your desires into reality.

Shift Your Perspective: On Regret

How many times have you wished that you had or had not done something? How often do you fantasize about making different choices and where you would be today if you had chosen an alternate path? Do you pine for the good old days? Does regret sometimes set in?

Next time you feel like that, consider this: everything is related. If you connect the dots between all of your experiences throughout your life, you see how necessary each step was to get to the next phase, and the one after that. Even when it seems like there were times when you could have been doing something more productive, connect that experience to what it taught you and allowed you to do down the road.

For example, you found something as an adult that you wish you had begun much sooner so you could have been further along by now. The truth is that you were not ready until now. Relate the events in your life and see how each experience has contributed to moving you forward.

It is hard to shift out of the sense of "if only I had/had not..." fill in the blank:

- If only I had not spent so much time in that unhealthy relationship
- If only I had not spent too much money partying and shopping
- If only I had studied in school or pursued that degree
- If only I had not treated someone so poorly

... the list is endless.

The energy of regret can hold you back, create guilt and self-loathing, and limit your ability to see what is possible going forward. Accept the choices you made. Acknowledge that the decision was based on what you wanted and your state of mind at the time. From that perspective, it is unlikely that you would have been able to see different options available to you.

It is easy to look back and criticize yourself and your choices. As the saying goes, "Hindsight is 20/20." You can see clearly into the past and evaluate the results of behaviors and choices that, today, you would have an entirely different outlook on. Those choices made as a teenager were coming from a teen mind, not the mature person you are today.

Knowing what you know now, the view is quite broader, your options are expanded, and your foresight is more developed. You understand consequences and the idea of *if I do this, then that is going to happen.* Also, you can envision the longer term result. As a teen who liked to tan, did you think the wrinkles from the sun would show up so prominently as you aged? Did you care about the future, or did you just want to look good in the moment? Yes, that is a small example, but with far-reaching effects on your appearance.

So now that you have gained experience, knowledge, and the wisdom that results when combining the two, what choices will you make going forward? Are you stuck in a continuous loop of similar choices that create regret, or do you consider the effect today's decisions have in the future? Even in adulthood, the view is based on the present level of understanding.

An important lesson is how to live life in a way that promotes peace and tranquility rather than anxiety and stress. Two choices you can make for the good of your present and your future are 1) living in alignment with your true nature, and 2) removing the stressors that muddle your thinking and hurt you emotionally.

You cannot go back and change the things you regret, but you can use those moments to learn valuable lessons to change your thoughts, behaviors, and decision-making process in order make better choices going forward. Life is a series of learning opportunities. Be at peace with where you are now.

From whatever vantage point you are at right now, think about how you want to look back on your life and what you represented in the world. Staying in energetic alignment with that vision will ensure that you have very little to regret.

Exercise 1-16: Make a chronological list of significant phases in your life where you feel regret. Include personal, school, and work circumstances and the way you chose to live those moments. Now connect each one to a belief, attitude, or behavior that exists in your life today. Did those times move you forward as far as level of understanding, or is there still more work to do to benefit from those experiences? How did those times change your perspective and in what way? What can you change today as a result of an experience you regret from the past? Example: Not pursuing a degree years ago can lead to returning to school or doing more reading in your field of interest and having a greater appreciation of the material than you would have had at a younger age.

The key to a joyous life is to live without regret. Regret for the things you have done or have not done. Regret for not spending that extra moment with a loved one or saying yes to something that was not in your best interest.

Make choices that drive you forward and that do not end in regret. Enjoy the things you have and be grateful for all that is in your life. Do not focus on regrets from the past, but rather look around you and find the beauty, the love, and the opportunities that create the future you desire.

Enjoy the time you have. Each moment of life is precious; make the most of it. When mistakes happen, learn from them. Tell the people you care about how you feel about them. Try to uplift those around you; make it so that people are happy to see you. Be in high service to others and look for opportunities to lighten someone's mood.

When that long-awaited insight or situation finally happens, avoid regret that it did not happen sooner. Everything happens when it is supposed to, in the perfect time, when you are truly ready to get the most out of it.

Shift Your Perspective: On Toxic Emotions

Happiness eludes those who harbor toxic emotions. If you are looking for peace in your life, nothing can disrupt that goal faster than harboring toxic emotions. Hate, fear, and envy are a few that take a toll on your peace of mind and on your relationships. Many times these three go hand-in-hand. William Penn said, "The jealous are troublesome to others, but a torment to themselves."

Jealousy is a low-level energy with detrimental impact. When you feel jealous toward someone for what she has or for her accomplishments, take a hard look at the source of what you are feeling. It could be stemming from a sense of inadequacy or self-doubt that makes you feel unable to accomplish your goals. The person you are jealous of might or might not have what you want, but the sheer success someone else is experiencing may be enough to trigger your disdain.

Exercise 1-17: Identify a toxic emotion you have been living with and determine its source. When did it begin? What triggered it? What perpetuates it? What effect is it having on your relationships and your life in general? Now challenge the notion that this emotion is justified. It may be that a former partner cheated on you, so now suspicion marks all of your relationships. Once you have confirmed that your partner is in fact faithful, explore what is keeping the fear alive. If the jealousy is perpetuated by the fear of losing the current partner, then know that nothing pushes away a significant other faster than erroneous accusations. Talk through the fears with your partner and journal about any inadequacies you harbor. Get professional assistance if needed.

Letting go of jealousy, hate, and fear opens a space for fresh energy to come in. Do so by bolstering self-esteem, working on accomplishing a unique goal, and being happy for those who are accomplishing their dreams. In this way, you enrich your own life and get closer to feeling a sense of inner peace. All of this is possible when the energy spent on negative attention toward another is suspended. You can recapture that energy and use it for the highest good.

Shift Your Perspective: On Yourself

The work starts with the Self. In astrology, the first house is that of the Self. In tarot, its images show you the journey of the Self and the way to deeper understanding. In *The Book of Runes*, Ralph Blum calls it "The Oracle of the Self." In metaphysical philosophy, The Great Work is the work of the Self, and its tenets and techniques are designed to go deep into self-discovery to strengthen one's gifts and to address one's weaknesses. The Work is one that results in freedom from anxiety, detachment from outcomes, trust in the Universe or natural process, deep self-awareness, and mindfulness of the present state of being.

It is a treacherous and fearsome journey to dive deep into the hidden crevices and shadowy places where you tuck away upsetting experiences, hurt feelings, and self-doubt. They can remain in the darkness for a lifetime, or you can step into your power and unveil them as lessons, thereby taking away their hold on you. Clearing these pain points is essential to being an adept, to gaining self-confidence, and to opening up to learning the next set of lessons. The work of the Self is never done. You can take it on as a great adventure or shy away from it.

What is your true nature? It is not the role you play or the circumstances that keep you blocked. It is the core of your being where your Inner Magick lives. It is the place that sets you apart and allows you to express your uniqueness. It differentiates you from all of the other trees in the forest.

Knowing the nature of your special gifts, your Inner Magick, transforms you from a follower to a unique individual living his or her life purpose. You came into this life to walk a path that is yours alone. At the same time, the path does include interacting with others, for through our relationships, we discover our true nature.

We tend to focus on expressions of love toward someone we care about, that is, someone external to ourselves. The depth of love you are able to bestow on others correlates with the amount of love you give yourself. Without self-love, there is the potential to allow others to take advantage of you, take you for granted, or manipulate or control you.

Those around you are reflections of what you think of yourself and what you believe you bring to the world. If your relationships are filled with strife, then you are out of sync with your true self. You are attempting to be what others want you to be. If your relationships are loving and supportive, they are reflecting the expression of who you truly are. When you align your energies with what you are at the core, things are easier, opportunities open, and the right people and situations come into your life. Your stress is minimized and joy is more prevalent than worry.

When you love yourself, and this is not conceit that we are talking about here, you avoid people and things that make you feel anxious, depressed, or drained. You take care of your body by exercising and eating nutritious foods. You are grateful for all of the things going right with your body, heart, mind, and life. You talk to yourself in a loving, caring way, instead of a barrage of negative self-talk that lowers your self-esteem. You stop complaining and start looking for the things that make you happy.

Exercise 1-18: Starting today, vow to be devoted to loving and caring for yourself now and always. Spend quality time with yourself and get to know who you are and what matters to you. Improve your relationship with yourself and watch how your external relationships change for the better. Respect and love yourself and you will attract love and respect in all of your relationships.

If you continue to struggle with the same things as you did years ago, take a look at what is creating the difficulty. Have you maintained the notion that you are unable to handle the situation or that you are powerless? What other ideas relating to how you view yourself are perpetuating the struggles in your life? Is there a particular focus, such as relationships or self-worth? Write down the issues that have lasted for several years or more, and then write down all of the thoughts you have about yourself that prevent you from addressing them. This will point you to the self-image that is holding you back.

With every thought and decision, you engage in a constant conversation with yourself. What you say in this self-talk can raise or lower your vibrational frequency. It can determine what you accomplish or shy away from. The opinions you have about yourself can foster confidence or self-doubt.

When you feel incapable, you put stress on yourself. Remember times in your youth when things were difficult, when you faced challenges that today would be easily overcome. The circumstances did not change, but rather, your idea of what you are capable of has shifted. Your experience has expanded, and along with it, your capabilities.

In each case, you are letting the Universe know how you feel and what you think of yourself. What you receive and manifest is directly related to this. If you feel like nothing is going right for you, and your self-talk is an incessant reminder to yourself and the Universe that nothing can go right for you, the dark cloud will continue to follow you. If, despite some obstacle, you believe that things work out for the best and you tell yourself that everything happens for a reason, it displays trust in the process of the Universe.

Here is how you can align and partner with the Universe to create the life and reality you want for yourself. When asking for something specific, ask for it to manifest in the highest good, giving the Universe permission to block or delay the request if it deems necessary. Not everything desired will have a positive outcome. Additionally, delays can prove beneficial, and only the Universe knows the best timing.

If shifting proves difficult, it may be a case of functional fixedness. Functional Fixedness is a term used in Cognitive Psychology that refers to a cognitive bias, wherein the perception of an object's function is limited only to its traditional use.

For example, in an experiment by Duncker (1945), subjects were tasked with mounting a candle on a door but not told how to do it. They were given a box of tacks, some matches, and the candle. It presented a difficult problem since most subjects saw the box as a container, rather than a platform, especially when filled with tacks. The person could not think to use the box in a way other than in its conventional function. This lack of mental flexibility creates a block to see things in ways beyond the original intention, and it limits problem-solving ability. It limits original thought and the ability to generate alternatives when looking at your options. Additionally, it keeps you stuck in how you see life or a particular circumstance.

Exercise 1-19: Shift your perspective by practicing ways to overcome functional fixedness. Take objects from around the house that you have only ever used for a particular purpose. Look at the objects one at a time and write down as many novel or non-conventional ways to use the object as you can. It may be difficult at first, but the more you do it, the more broadly you will begin to perceive things in your environment. Your mind will begin to work in more expansive ways when problem solving, and you will see your imagination blossom. Doing this will lead you into a realm of expansive awareness, and you will be amazed by how your perception of the world, and yourself, will change.

Now take a particular life event. For example, you get laid off from a job. How many ways can you view this occurrence? Without editing yourself, list everything that comes to mind. This exercise can be performed with any situation, especially those that create initial disappointment or upset. Back to the job example; it could be viewed as your former employer never appreciated you or your work, as fearful that another job will not come along, as relief because you did not like that job anyway, or as a great opportunity to try something new. Each perspective creates a different response—respectively, depression, fear, relief, excitement. By shifting your view of the situation, your opportunity for happiness increases or declines.

Stay mindful of how you view yourself and your circumstances. Your best opportunities for happiness are right in front of you.

Chapter 2: Regarding the External

Shift Your Perspective: On Acceptance

Fighting against what you have no control over and resisting change is exhausting. Whether you are fighting with your family, a perceived enemy, or in some long-term legal battle, fighting can wear you down. The energy being directed at the battle is better used to bring your visions to life. Even being in a situation where you energetically have to protect yourself the entire time (like at work or with certain people) is exhausting. Your exhaustion decreases your tolerance level and increases your anxiety. So what to do instead?

Accept those things you cannot control and take responsibility for the things you can. Allow changes to take place, and let go of the things that no longer serve you. Activities, relationships, and thought patterns that make you feel tired and agitated need to be eliminated. These you have control over; you choose to participate or not.

When it is time for a relationship or way of being to end, accept that the end is a natural part of the growth cycle. Change is necessary and constant. Accepting that and taking advantage of opportunities that come with change is energizing and cultivates peace in your life.

Stop fighting and resisting. Either accept what is in your life or take charge and change it.

> **Exercise 2-1:** Make two columns and list the things you are fighting against. Next to each one place a "C" for "have control over it" or an "N" for "have no control over it." For each item marked with "N," let go of the fight and accept it or change it. Try addressing one "N" per week.

Shift Your Perspective: On Aging

Many of the women I enjoy spending time with are in their later years—the time after the feminine cycle has ceased and the wisdom of experience has ripened. They use what they have learned and continue to seek out new adventures. A large number of them seek to discover themselves anew in the context of their later years. Their self-concept shifts as the focus moves away from spouse, children, and career. A new adventure presents itself, and ways in which to express their true nature come forward. What inspires us in our later years is different than in the middle or mother phase of life. We still create, yet the motivation changes. Seeking inner peace, harmony in relationships, and a true sense of self become the keys and purpose.

Evolved women in their mature years recognize what wastes their time and energy much more quickly than when they are in their youth or mother phases. They seek out positive, peaceful people and know that self-care is just as important as taking care of everyone else. These women understand the lesson of being kind to themselves when enduring difficult periods, knowing that it is just a temporary circumstance that will pass as all other troubles have. Those who are stuck in old patterns and have difficulty finding their way can benefit by finding alliances with mature women who have successfully navigated life to this juncture in order to change from a sense of disappointment and negativity to feeling inspired and hopeful.

I highly value the beauty, love, joy, and wisdom that mature women bring to my life. At the same time, I admire their willingness to try new things, step out of their comfort zones, and seek out new experiences, while enjoying the ride. I even find myself at the most contented point in my life, where gratitude permeates the everyday blessings, a learning opportunity is around every corner, and my goals are focused on evolving my creative expression. Aging is a beautiful gift that gives us opportunities not available to us in youth. Notice the growth process at every stage of life and take advantage of what each has to offer.

Exercise 2-2: Identify a mature woman you admire. Notice how she moves through life and how her philosophy guides her actions. Listen to stories of how she was in youth and the process she went through to gain wisdom and self-trust. Take what you learn from her and apply it to your own life. If you are already at this stage, take the time to teach others who are interested in growing and developing.

Shift Your Perspective: On Clarity

Nothing is more anxiety-provoking than being in limbo, that sense of uncertainty and not knowing what you want or how to go about getting what you want. This time is when clarity is key; getting crystal clear about your motivations, your life purpose, and what you want your life to look like can transform anxiety and procrastination into purposeful action. Going from the familiar daily grind and feeling like nothing can change to understanding that you have the power to create whatever you want can cause some to avoid changing the way they look at their lives. It can be scary to envision a completely different way of being. It will create changes in your relationships, your work, and in your self-image. Yet, when you realize that this new way will bring you the happiness, passion, and motivation that you have always wanted, the task becomes exciting!

Exercise 2-3: Begin by writing down everything you would like to have in your life—the type of work, relationships, money, residence, activities, etc. Do this with abandon—do not edit yourself, and do not place restrictions on what is possible. Avoid the standard "winning the lottery" vision, and instead, ask yourself, "If there were no barriers, how would I want to live my life?"

Write as much as you can think of; then review the list. What are the patterns you see? What type of people are around you in your new vision? What are you doing with your life? Now that there is clarity, begin to make gradual changes to move toward that vision. Practice acting "as if" it were already your reality. The clearer the vision, the greater the ability to manifest your desires.

Shift Your Perspective: On Competition

The word "competition" conjures a sense of going up against someone to win, to show that you are better than another. It implies the need to defeat another. To me, crushing the self-esteem of an opponent lessens the experience of winning. Another way to approach this concept is to understand it in light of an opportunity for personal development. Viewing it from this perspective frees us from making someone else feel lesser in his or her skills and abilities. My definition of healthy competition is being in competition with yourself instead of with others. Do not measure yourself against anyone but yourself.

Other people have different gifts and approaches than you do. You are on different paths, possibly using similar abilities. Both have value.

Exercise 2-4: In the case of wanting to improve your skills at something, play or work with someone who has achieved a high level of ability in that area. Say you want to get better at playing a game such as pool. Playing against and watching those who are expert is an excellent way of developing your own skills.

You may never catch up to someone else's level, but you will improve and learn each time you play the person. Go in with the mindset of playing against yourself and exceeding your personal best. Did you sink more balls this time? Were you able to use English on the cue ball more accurately? When the answer is yes, be proud to have achieved beyond your original skill level. You have "won," even if the person you are playing scored more points than you did.

When playing someone who is not yet up to your skill level, be humble and assist in his or her learning. In this way, great satisfaction will be experienced by all.

Shift Your Perspective: On Complaining

We have a choice in the type of energy that fills our lives. Those who take every opportunity to complain about what they have or do not have bring low-level, dense energy into their lives. The presence of this type of energy serves to attract more of the same, creating an endless cycle of things to moan about.

At that point, this perspective becomes habitual and seeps into every aspect of life, and the person experiences a sense of unease that eventually becomes pessimism. From this juncture, it is difficult to generate alternatives and get motivated to make necessary changes toward leading a happy life. What is the use? Nothing will go right, anyway.

On the other hand, if that same person took the opportunity to look for the lesson held within each circumstance and consider it as a necessary step to reach the next level, the response contains a much higher frequency. At higher vibrational levels, the individual experiences an uplifting energy he can use to expand his options.

With each shift from feeling unfortunate to feeling grateful for the experience, the energy heightens and pulls in increasingly better situations that increase the likelihood of manifesting the desired lifestyle. Let go of past issues so you can immediately feel lighter and more hopeful.

Be mindful of the type of energy permeating every aspect of life and intentionally raise its frequency with gratitude, insight, and openness to the possibilities held within.

Exercise 2-5: Ask your friends to alert you when you start complaining about something. Having it brought to awareness allows the opportunity to stop complaining immediately. Start realizing when you hear yourself complain, and then stop, take a deep breath, and shift the complaint into how you plan to address the problem.

Shift Your Perspective: On Detachment

You have hear the word, "detachment," but you haven't found a way to apply this important concept. Let us start by defining it and discovering the way its antithesis, "attachment," can manifest in your life.

Detachment simply means to remove emotionality regarding an outcome, to unplug the drama and the attachment to a particular person or circumstance. While the definition is simple, the ability to accomplish detachment is not.

Attachment, on the other hand, is commonplace. The desire or need to connect and control creates attachments. Deeply ingrained beliefs drive attachment and result in a perspective that seeks to validate that belief.

For example, the victim mindset manifests in anger and resentment as the individual holding this belief sees herself taken advantage of. Victimhood is a choice, and to shift this notion from suffering to boundary setting allows a sense of control. Blaming others serves to give away one's power. Responsibility enables one to stand in her power.

Attachment often coincides with the idea of caring. If you are mad, worried, or frustrated, then it demonstrates a sense of caring about the relationship or situation. Detachment is falsely associated with lack of concern. Associating detachment with trust that everything works out for the best allows a release of suffering over outcomes.

Release creates a wonderful space for new energy to come in. Yet the fear of what the old feeling might be replaced with is what prevents relinquishment in the first place. What would life be like without the distress that has become an integral part of life? It becomes lighter, freer, and happier; it allows for giving up of control and all the tension that goes along with it; it promotes inner peace and external harmony. It allows you to reclaim your life.

And despite these benefits, detachment still eludes the majority of folks.

Exercise 2-6: To get started on the path of detachment:

1. Select a relationship or situation.

2. Jot down the primary fear/anger/frustration associated with it, such as [insert name of family member or significant other here] does not love/respect/care about me.

3. Then ask yourself what drives these feelings. Is it that the person asks for favors without concern for the way you feel or how it impacts your life?

4. Now identify the role you play in the scenario. Do you say yes when you want to say no? Do you play the part of the victim who is always put upon? 5. Do you place blame on others for how you are feeling?
Then ask yourself what the reward is in maintaining this feeling. Do you seek sympathy, acknowledgment, or approval? Any behavior that persists is reinforced by a reward of some type, even though the ultimate result is emotional pain. Pinpoint the reward, and it will be easier to identify the source of the attachment.

6. Decide whether the reward causes discomfort or joy. If discomfort, determine what beliefs or behaviors of yours, not the other person's, need to change.

7. Practice new behaviors in accordance with the situation. If you say yes when you want to say no, then learn strategies to do so diplomatically, and set appropriate boundaries.

The above examples are ones I have seen played out over and over among hundreds of people. The real threat to your happiness and inner peace is unique to you and needs to be identified and shifted if you want to achieve happiness in your life. It requires a combination of changes in behavior, beliefs, and desires to create lasting change in relationships and circumstances.

Decide that you are ready for your life to be different and in what way, embody joyful detachment, and see what it feels like to allow your life to unfold easily as you give up the pain and drama of attachment.

Shift Your Perspective: On Disruption

Disruption is a catalyst for change, clearing out the old and making room for fresh new energy to come in. Each time your regular routine or thought process is interrupted, you have the opportunity to take a new approach to your life. Disturbances force change and are great opportunities to surmount obstacles and break destructive patterns.

Things like loss of a loved one, a job, losing or gaining a pet, or experiencing an illness, are examples of extreme disruptions that can create sweeping changes in the way you think, feel, behave, and live your life. Other types of occurrences may be less intense, but they can still cause significant disorder. Learning something profound changes your core beliefs and, ultimately, your understanding of yourself and your life. Having your car break down forces you to problem solve and change the way you look at transportation needs. The more severe the disruption, the more timely it is for your growth. Your reaction to the disruption is an indicator of the core issue it is there to reveal. The reaction serves to break old patterns.

Disruption calls attention to something that may be taken for granted. It breaks the humdrum routines that make us complacent and reluctant to take action. If you have drifted in indecision for too long, disruption can serve to force a decision to be made or to have the Universe make a decision for us.

Disruption brings our vulnerabilities to the forefront so they can be addressed. It shakes us out of our comfort zone and purges our preconceptions. It helps us to break free of constraints.

Exercise 2-7: Set a goal and define the type of change you want to create; the intention is to disrupt your old habit and create a new one. When setting the intention, be clear and specific about the goal you are setting. Do not just say, "I'll cut down on how much I'm eating, but rather, "I will not eat anything that is fried." Do not say, "I'll meditate more often," but rather, "I'll meditate for ten minutes each day." That way you know when you are off track, and it is easier to monitor your progress. Break your habit down into its smallest components, and then remove bits of them to disrupt its effect.

Shift Your Perspective: On Drama

People can be very emotional and reactive, and it is easy to get caught up in the drama of the situation. Responding to an emotional reaction with yet another emotional reaction just perpetuates the problem and heightens the ill feelings that may result.

Instead, try detaching from the situation and view it objectively. Rather than taking it personally, consider that the person may be reacting to something that the situation triggered deep within her. It may be that what she is reacting to is a lack of confidence or some other personal issue. I have seen people react to minor comments or situations because they have nothing else in their lives to focus on, and so they grab onto minutia and make it bigger than it needs to be.

Try letting go of the situation and understanding what is actually happening. Detachment does not mean you do not care, but rather, it removes the emotionality from the situation so it can be seen clearly. In this way, the lessons inherent in the situation may be gleaned without emotional upset. Practice detachment and see how much less drama you attract to your relationships.

It may be that your primary enemy takes the form of living with ever-present drama and guilt. The sense that you have committed an offense or feel responsible for the happiness of others is the root of guilt. This leads to the inevitable drama, where emotions run high, accusations are made, and then you may find it easiest to submit to another's will. There can be no drama without human interaction. Unless you are a hermit who lives on a mountain, there is a good chance that within your relationships you also experience drama and guilt. People stay in bad relationships out of guilt. People can try to manipulate you through guilt. Getting caught up in high emotionality with people who thrive on drama depletes your energy by demanding your attention.

This attention escalates the negativity and blocks intuitive messages that are telling you to let it all go and trust that there is a better way. All of this distracts from core changes and the need to see the situation objectively so that emotionality can be minimized.

The perpetuation of drama and guilt diminishes your energy and makes you feel tired, edgy, agitated, and easily upset. You worry that if you change and decide to take care of yourself first, the people around you will fall away from your life or they will be mad at you. When in the throes of a situation ripe with drama and guilt, there is a tendency to ignore the idea that people who want to control and manipulate you do not have your best interest at heart.

There is a real risk of losing yourself in an effort to maintain unhealthy relationships. You get to the point where you do not know who you are anymore; your identity is dependent upon what others need from you and want you to be for them. These types of relationships allow others to remain in power and inhibit your Inner Magick.

What are your current relationships trying to tell you about who you are? Relationships are reflections of who you are. Look at the quality of your relationships; how others treat you mirrors how you feel about yourself. You attract what you are and the situations that are the lessons you need to learn.

Your current relationships could be reflecting your fear of rejection, of saying the wrong thing, of being criticized, of not being liked, of hurting someone else's feelings, of being judged. They may be demonstrating your desire for acceptance from outside sources rather than from within yourself. They are there to mirror back your doubts so you can overcome them. Use them as a tool to change your perspective, overcome fears and doubts, and enhance your overall self-image.

Is what you are seeing what you truly think you are? If not, it is time to come into your true self. Here are some strategies to get started.

Exercise 2-8: Keys to Removing the Drama

1. Decide that you want things to be different. This is the first step toward change. Align your heart and your head; just saying you want things to be different doesn't make it so; coming into your power means deciding that things can and need to be different.

2. Release old beliefs and negative thoughts and emotions. Sometimes, you even need to release old relationships that no longer serve you. This is scary. And you do not want to hurt anybody, but keep in mind that the way it is now hurts you.

3. Set boundaries—say no when it is something that does not fit into your schedule or it is something you really do not want to do. This will alleviate resentment.

4. Give people back responsibility for themselves. By caretaking and enabling, spiritually and karmically, you are overstepping your boundaries and inserting yourself into someone else's path so that the person never learns his or her own life lessons and has the opportunity to grow.

5. Take care of yourself—By taking steps to look good and getting the right sleep, exercise, and nutrition, you will have higher energy and a positive outlook.

6. Refuse to participate in arguments, angst, complaining, or gossiping.

---

7. Detach emotionally. When you are emotionally attached to the situation, it is difficult to see how it is affecting you. It is possible to take an objective look at the situation by becoming a detached observer without the emotion so you can see what is really happening in the relationship. No emotion = no drama.

Shift Your Perspective: On Eating

There are those who use food as a hobby, as a stress-reduction strategy, for comfort, or to fill the void of what is missing from their lives. In actuality, food is not meant to replace other life experiences nor to act as an anti-anxiety or anti-depressant drug. That said, food is a chemical that interacts with the body in profound ways. Food is fuel that has the potential to promote the highest energy level, health benefits, and maximum cognitive functioning if properly used. Think about what happens when you eat a meal with a high fat content. Almost immediately, you begin to feel sluggish and unmotivated. The same goes for junk food and fast food.

Lack of proper nutrition exacerbates depression and anxiety, increases likelihood of illness, and lowers the energy available to use toward living a meaningful, productive life. The reverse is true when you eat a balanced meal of lean protein, complex carbohydrates, and fruits and vegetables. The result is high energy and a clear head, which are essential components of transformation and happiness. Health impacts the level of happiness experienced.

Exercise 2-9: Consider what you have been eating lately and take note of how you feel. Remove one unhealthy food choice per week and add a fruit or vegetable to your diet. Notice changes in energy, digestion, and mental clarity. This is one more spoke in your self-awareness wheel.

Unless you are already diligent about eating well, change the way you select food to reap the rewards of health, experience lower incidence of illness and disease, and enjoy high mental functioning. Better health translates into the ability to get more done, to feel good about yourself, and to stay on the path of healthy eating.

Rather than going on fad diets and consuming processed foods that make weight, sugar, and cholesterol levels fluctuate, choose fresh, whole foods. Consuming a consistently healthy diet creates ease of maintaining beneficial eating choices. For those challenged with weight loss, making healthy eating a lifestyle choice takes the emphasis off of measuring and depriving yourself of the things you enjoy and places it on nutrition. Having a treat is fine; balance is the key.

When used to eating properly, the body responds negatively any time you fall back into unhealthy eating habits, which results in a heightened awareness of the detriments of fatty, salty, sugary foods on your mind and body. Yes, we are spiritual beings, our core is energy, but we live on the physical plane, so it is essential to take care of the one body you get in this lifetime.

Shift Your Perspective: On Encouragement

If you have ever played the computer game Bejeweled, you have experienced its built-in encouragement and praise. Each time you make a good move, a powerful voice accompanies the words emblazoned on the screen: good, excellent, awesome, and spectacular, with exciting sounds and visuals that make you want to keep playing.

Encouragement helps you to press on, even when the going gets tough. Having someone tell you that you can do it, or that he believes in you, helps you muster the fortitude needed to get to the final goal.

In some ways, encouragement is synonymous with faith; when someone believes in you and has faith that you are capable of accomplishing what you set out to do, it is more likely that you will believe in yourself. Having that extra boost when fatigue or doubt sets in gets you over the hump and provides support and hope for the future. It can also come across as approval during times when uncertainty creeps in. Encouragement is a verbal pat on the back.

Knowing how good it feels to be encouraged yourself, turning it toward others can make a major difference in someone else's life. Letting someone know you believe in her can help that person achieve her goals or rekindle her faith in herself. It is a powerful gesture. It can enhance her self-esteem and open her to wanting to strive harder. Supportive words may be just what the person needs to overcome a moment of discomfort, change an unhealthy behavior, complete a course of study, finish a special project, or begin a journey that will help her create the life she truly wants.

It is also possible to encourage yourself by getting in touch with what motivates you and seeing how what you are striving for aligns with that. Encouragement in this regard is necessary when inspiration wanes.

Exercise 2-10: When you feel like you are running out of steam, take a step back and reevaluate your action plan and your reasons for being on a particular path. Have the reasons changed? Have your goals been modified? Have you discovered something about yourself that calls you to transition into a new way of being? What is it that you are trying to be or do?

Encourage yourself and recognize that you know yourself best. Do not allow yourself to be discouraged. Seek out those who will encourage you to accomplish what you want in your life, and look for opportunities to encourage others to step into their own greatness.

Shift Your Perspective: On Forgiveness

There is a difference between forgiveness and acceptance. I was speaking with a woman who told me she has been depressed and miserable over an upheaval with a family member. The situation had caused a rift in the family and, as a result, she was unable to move forward in her life. Her friend advised her to forgive the relative who had caused this problem. Now she was struggling with trying to find the ability to forgive him and was exhausted from the effort. Her new mantra became, *If only I could forgive him.*

There is evidence that forgiveness enables the victimized person to release negative emotions toward the violator and to get on with life. The act of forgiveness also holds hope that the person being forgiven will make amends and transform in some way that will be to his or her benefit. The decision to release resentment toward someone who has harmed you can result in lowered blood pressure and increased compassion toward the offender.

Forgiveness assumes that the offender wants to be forgiven or that he feels he has done something to warrant being forgiven. While that is not always true, the person may feel completely justified in his actions or have an impairment that prevents the realization of wrongdoing. Within forgiveness is contained aspects of guilt, remorse, judgment, worry, doubt, blame, and submission. The person you are forgiving may or may not feel any of those things. Forgiveness takes energy and requires a specific action on the part of the person who has been "wronged" toward a person he or she has judged to be in error.

On the other hand, acceptance requires only that the person who feels hurt examines what it is about the situation that is creating this reaction. By doing so, it promotes insight into the self and affords the opportunity to base the next action on your own highest good. It may be time to end the destructive pattern created by the relationship with the other person and so the decision would involve separation without judgment. If you can understand the lesson held within the interaction, then judgment ceases and you are able to move beyond the negative energy. While there is resolve, release, and closure to the "victim" in forgiveness, the act of acceptance promotes personal power and growth.

Exercise 2-11: Rather than tormenting yourself over "why" someone did what he did, accept that it is part of his path and that you only have control over your own path. You have the power to make your path the best it can be. If there is an obstacle that cannot be moved, go around it, adjust your actions, and transcend the issue through your own development.

Acceptance brings inner peace, for there is no guilt or judgment involved. It allows one to see the lessons inherent in the situation and the growth opportunities it presents. Rather than forgiveness, acceptance gives you back control over your own life by removing the power someone else's actions have over you. It is not about what the person did, but how you respond to it, how you grow from it, and what you learn from it.

Shift Your Perspective: On Getting Help

There's a lot to be said for taking responsibility for yourself and achieving your goals. At the same time, trying to do everything yourself is exhausting and fruitless. Enlisting the help you need to take care of the mundane chores that should be shared leaves you more time to pursue the things only you can focus on. It does not take away from your independence or make you any less of a superhero. It does, however, acknowledge the value you bring to the situation when your focus is on your unique gifts.

For example, getting help with cleaning the house from others who live with you or hiring someone to help with that takes a huge load off of you and enables you to focus on what will get you closer to what you want. I know many people who have a giant list of activities that need to be accomplished, complain that they have no time to do anything worthwhile, and spin their wheels trying to get it all done—ultimately running in place and getting no farther than when they started.

Getting help also applies when you are on a hamster wheel of the same thoughts and perspectives. It is difficult to self-observe and gain alternate views on a situation without viewpoints that can only come from others. Find trustworthy sources who can be objective as the circumstances' various aspects are discussed. Consult professionals for help in moving past particularly difficult roadblocks, keeping in mind that doing so is not a sign of weakness, but rather that you place value on your wellbeing and are comfortable taking steps to resolve outstanding issues.

Exercise 2-12: Set your goals and then make a list of everything required to achieve them. Then make a list of everything else you need to take care of in your life. Outsource anything that does not look like something *only you* can do. Get help and see how much farther you get. You will be less stressed, the creative juices will be flowing, and you will be more successful overall.

Shift Your Perspective: On Gratification

We have become a society of instant gratification. We want immediate certifications for courses of study that rightly should take years, we want to lose ten pounds in a week, and we want a pill that will get rid of what ails us. If the desired result does not happen immediately, it results in anger, frustration, and low self-esteem. A giving up response soon follows, feeling as though the effort to get what is desired is not worth it.

The satisfaction level associated with instant gratification is temporary, such as in retail therapy. The excitement experienced with the purchase of that new outfit is short-lived, requiring another shopping excursion to fill the void.

The truth is that instant gratification is not possible in most cases; it requires work and time to develop. When you plant a seed, it does not sprout overnight. When the desired result requires effort and time to develop, at the moment when the ultimate outcome is achieved, the payoff is much greater and includes long-term satisfaction. Delayed gratification is the key to true fulfillment and happiness.

Delayed gratification also creates something to look forward to. With instantaneous results, it is necessary to continue to find the next desire and then the next and the next. By working toward something over time, each milestone brings its own sense of accomplishment, with the ultimate goal bringing the biggest reward of all—confidence, self-trust, and self-esteem.

Long-term gratification requires self-control and self-discipline to stay the course. Tenacity enables you to complete what you start. When the momentum is arrested and the activity halted, the likelihood of completing the necessary steps to reach the goal diminishes. The act of starting something new each time frustration enters onto the path results in never completing the original goal. When multiple unfinished projects are in the works, motivation is reduced and self-doubt takes over.

Exercise 2-13: Select one unfinished project on your list. It could be something as simple as finishing the book that has been sitting on your nightstand for the last six months. It can be large or small, short-term or long-term. How long has it lingered? Is it still something that is meaningful to you? Would you feel great satisfaction if it were completed?

Now write down the reasons why this project's completion would bring gratification, followed by specific steps needed to bring it to completion, including getting whatever help is required. Set a reasonable timeline with a specific due date for each step, including the final due date. Stick to the timeline and cultivate self-discipline to adhere to the due dates. Give yourself a pat on the back when the project is completed. Note the level of satisfaction and happiness you feel at the end of the project.

Shift Your Perspective: On Judgment

Judgment is a debilitating practice—whether the judgment is toward others or toward yourself. It happens whenever you label someone in a general way. It is a snap evaluation of that person based on your past experiences and core beliefs. You draw a conclusion about something before knowing all the facts or considering it within the context of the situation. It is merely your perception of that person, and not the only truth.

When you judge others, it serves to close you off from a connection with that person and from the lesson held within that interaction. Whether it is about the actions, beliefs, or efforts of another, judging serves to limit understanding. It also directs negativity at that person. Live and let live to avoid judgment.

Exercise 2-14: When evaluating a person or circumstance, determine whether it is your intention to send that person negativity or understanding. How is what the person is saying or doing striking a chord for you that creates a judgmental stance? Is the judgment a result of what you have been taught to believe? Practice other ways of looking at it.

It is the same when you point that judgment at yourself—that negative self-talk that arises with generalized statements such as, "Man, you are so stupid," or "I should have known better," or the ever popular, "I can't do anything right." Now you are sending negativity to yourself!

This practice only serves to weaken you and lessen your ability to overcome challenges. Focus on the specific thing that just happened, the choice that was made, or the action taken. Now consider how you perceived it and remember that you are on a path of growth.

Maybe you just made a spontaneous choice that could have been given a bit more thought. Instead of calling yourself a disparaging name, tell yourself that the choice you made felt right in the moment and that next time, you will choose to give it additional thought before making a decision. That statement feels lighter, doesn't it?

How about when someone else is doing something that you do not approve of? Maybe she is living a lifestyle different from what you consider acceptable. Rather than judging, tell yourself that it is great to live in a country where a wide range of beliefs and lifestyles are possible. Or more specifically, thinking that the path she is on is what is right for her to learn the lessons she came here to complete. Acceptance holds a higher vibrational frequency.

Each person is on the journey he or she is on because he or she chose it. Allowing yourself and others to travel on the path without judgment is a supportive gesture that leaves room for differences and for mistakes, while giving unconditional acceptance.

Learning through experience and from interactions with others allows one to take command of the situation in a way that is for the highest good. Who is to say what is best for one person or another, except the person herself.

Rather than judging, try to understand the true nature of the person or the situation and, thereby, the lesson held within the interaction. Pay attention to the impact you have on others, as well as on yourself, and see what can be learned in the process. To each his own!

Shift Your Perspective: On Learning

Whenever we embark on the study of anything—to learn a skill, a concept, or a way of being—the learning helps us to transcend our understanding from where we are to a higher level. New knowledge challenges our current way of thinking, allowing us to question what we thought we knew, or to enhance the meaning of what we already know. We can build upon foundational concepts with ever more intricate aspects of a topic, adding dimension and depth.

Our brains physically transform, lighting up the neo-cortex and making new neural pathways to accommodate the information. We expand and open, seek and consider, dispute and accept, and in the end, come to a greater understanding of the topic and ourselves. Each time we open to new information or intensely study a particular topic, we become more self-aware, exploring the depths of what we believe and how we view the world.

We decide which bits of information to incorporate based on how it feels to us, as we determine whether it fits into our worldview or completely changes our perceptions. Our studies can lead us onto new pathways to follow a stream of philosophy or skill acquisition that is uncovered during the study of the original topic. Follow it along until you come to its end, and go down any tributaries you find interesting. You never know what awaits you until you check it out.

There is so much to learn in so many areas. Study what there is in your particular topic of interest, and then seek to contribute your unique gifts to the subject. Read widely until you know enough to form your own opinions. There is a reason you are attracted to certain learning opportunities, so explore why you are interested in the subject, how it fits in with your personal identity and self-concept, and in what ways it contributes to your self-awareness. Combat stagnation through reading, questioning, and contributing. Continuing education and study throughout your lifetime ensures perpetual growth and transformation.

Exercise 2-15: Try to learn something new every day. Apply what you learn to get the most out of the information and to assimilate the knowledge in a way that promotes wisdom.

Shift Your Perspective: On Meeting New People

When you always hang out with the same people, unless they are incredibly dynamic, you run the risk of stagnation. You hear the same opinions, you get the same perspectives, and you do not open yourself to new information. When you encounter new people, you get different reflections of yourself so that the depth of who you are can be revealed.

Exercise 2-16: When attending events, shopping, or at work, seek out new people. See how others react to you, listen to how others see the world, and attempt to discover something new.

Go to an event alone to increase your chances of talking to someone new. If you go with a friend, the likelihood of focusing on interactions with your friend is higher than talking to a new acquaintance. At the same time, having a friend along may increase your comfort level. Either way, set a goal to meet at least one new person and have a conversation.

If you need the support of a familiar person, make sure you open yourself to speaking to someone you have never met. This past weekend, I attended a conference alone for this very reason, and I met several new contacts who possess a depth of knowledge in certain areas I was seeking to learn more about. The interactions allowed me to expand my understanding and connected me to those who could help me with some projects. They are also very nice people! I'm looking forward to staying in touch and possibly working together in the future.

Look for opportunities to meet new people wherever you are and start growing from the experience.

Shift Your Perspective: On Obligation

How many times have you done things out of obligation instead of joy? An internal struggle occurs each time you make a decision based on *having* to do it versus *wanting* to do it. Guilt and resentment happen when you are manipulated into doing something by instilling a sense of duty or responsibility derived from someone else's needs rather than our own.

The next time you are faced with a choice, ask yourself whether it is something that feels good to you. An example would be to offer support to a friend who is going through a difficult time because you want to be there for that person, not because you feel you have to. Being an everyday hero can bring great joy into your life. In a world that can be disappointing, uncaring, and cruel, you can make a difference. It is easy to be an everyday hero. There are opportunities to reach out to others—both those you already know, as well as total strangers.

The grocery store is a great place to touch the life of someone. For example, I saw someone whose shoe was untied and she was having difficulty tying it due to a physical impairment. I asked whether I could help and tied it for her. Something so simple took her from distressed to calm. Someone actually took an interest and cared enough to help. She did not have to ask.

Hold the door open for those behind you at the store, help someone reach an item on the supermarket shelf, or let someone out onto the road in traffic. Be aware of how your actions affect others and take care to be considerate. Lend a hand to a neighbor shoveling snow. In our neighborhood, the able-bodied neighbors shovel the walks and driveways of the elderly residents nearby. Those who cannot shovel are grateful and feel cared for. To see the relief at not having to worry about how the snow will get removed is a wonderful reward, and the grateful neighbor gets joy from reciprocating with homemade cookies that bring happiness as well. There is no sense of obligation, but rather a focus on community support and high service to others that makes the interaction satisfying for all.

These simple acts of kindness shift the vibrational frequency up on both the giving and receiving end, and they promote more heroic acts as the kindness is paid forward and significantly increases happiness on both sides of the interaction.

On the other hand, if the doing for a particular person is a situation that occurs with regularity and expectation, and there is always a crisis to be dealt with, then make the decision based on how effective you will be in the situation. Are you rescuing this person over and over again? Is it time to hand the person back responsibility for him- or herself?

Doing what makes you feel good includes both personal and work life. To work out of joy and passion feels good; to work out of obligation creates dense, stuck energy. If you are not doing the work that makes you feel good, shift this feeling by deciding to approach your work with gratitude for providing money you need to live, or you can decide to change your occupation and pursue work that makes you feel good while providing a livelihood. It is all about the decisions you make and the reasons you make them. Choose the option that makes you feel good!

Exercise 2-17: Identify a situation where you have acted out of obligation and one where you acted out of kindness. How did you feel in each situation? What prompted you to take action when you felt obligated to do so? What was the underlying emotion—guilt, fear—and what was the resulting emotion afterward—resentment, fatigue? What inspired you to help someone out of kindness? How did you feel afterward—happy, energized?

Shift Your Perspective: On Rejection

Any time you reject a situation, outmoded belief, resentment, negative emotion, relationship, or pretty much anything that does not fit with your vision or what you want your life to look like, things change in miraculous ways. By doing this, you are clearing old energies so new opportunities can come into your life.

This even works when you purge your belongings and rid yourself of things associated with a time in your life that is no longer pertinent to your growth. For example, if you have lost weight and still hold onto clothes that no longer fit you, get rid of them. Reject the doubt of being able to maintain your new weight and remove the safety net your old clothes provide.

Make room for fresh ideas, behaviors, and situations that lead to your next level of development. There are times when being rejected by others can transform you by drawing your attention to where you need to improve, changes you may need to make, or types of relationships that are best for your wellbeing. Many times, being rejected by a certain organization or individual can be a blessing in disguise because removing that potentially damaging energy from your life would not have happened otherwise. In most cases, it is simply a matter of being out of energetic alignment with a particular person or group. It is not good nor bad; those associations are just inconsistent with your nature or your vision.

Exercise 2-18: Draw a line down the middle of a piece of paper or use your computer. Make a list of what you want in your life down one column, and in the other, list all of the things currently in your life that are preventing you from reaching your goals. Then remove/reject those things that no longer serve your vision. You will find that you are able to manifest your ideal life much more quickly without those low-level vibrations weighing you down.

Shift Your Perspective: On Relationships

Relationships... they are the foundation of our lives. Whether it is a relationship with a coworker, family member, friend, or significant other, the way we feel in our relationships with others has a lot to do with how we feel about ourselves.

So many people want to help others, take care of those around them, and do whatever is in their power to make life better for those they care about. They devote themselves to their children, spouse, job, parents, and friends, making sure their needs are met, no matter what has to be put aside, delayed, or denied for themselves.

We are all here to help each other in high service, to learn lessons, to lend support, to guide, to heal, and to understand ourselves within the context of others. But when that help results in exhaustion, anger, frustration, resentment, and sadness, it is time to take a hard look at what is happening. These are symptoms of losing yourself in the process of helping someone else.

Losing yourself occurs when your identity is eclipsed by those around you—when the definition of your life becomes what others need from you or the role you play in their lives. Uncertainty of who you are comes when your self-identity is tied to the perceived value you provide to others. For example, if the person you are helping has the opinion that you are not doing enough for him or that you are doing it in a less than optimum way, your self-esteem goes down, along with your confidence.

The thing is, no matter what you do for some people, it will never be enough. Let us face it; even with the best intentions, there are times when no amount of energy, worry, or stress can make a difference in the life of someone who is not allowed to take responsibility for himself. Granted, sometimes a person needs a leg up, a bolster during a time of need, to help him get back on his feet. When the situation turns into constant need of assistance from you, then it enters into the unhealthy zone.

If you are caretaking for an elderly family member or terminally ill person, that person's need will never be reduced, but there are still ways you can stay detached while giving the person the care he or she needs. Hand the reins over to someone else for an hour or two and do something just for yourself. Take a walk, soak in the tub surrounded by candles, read a book, watch your favorite program, or go out to eat. Seek to help others without losing yourself.

Exercise 2-19: Make a list of the relationships that require the most energy. Evaluate how much energy you are putting toward others in a subservient way. Is the demand for your attention such that you feel drained after helping? Do you feel tired and frustrated in the relationship? Do you get what you need from the interaction? Do you feel appreciated? If you find that you have lost yourself within the relationship, take steps to pull back or utilize additional resources in order to manage what the relationship requires.

For some, suggesting that you take time for yourself is an invitation to disaster. Feelings of being neglectful, uncaring, selfish, and the guilt that goes along with it, surface. If you do not take time for yourself and get what you need, you cannot possibly take care of anyone else. It is like in the airplane when the oxygen mask drops—put your mask on first and then help those around you. If you do not have any air, you will pass out and be unable to help others.

A healthy relationship is a balance of give and take, each person helping the other as needed, while taking responsibility for him- or herself at the same time. Each gets what he or she needs, not only one or the other. The Universe seeks energetic balance; it never meant for you to deplete yourself in service to others.

Shift Your Perspective: On Saying No

One of the hardest things you can do is to say no. How often do you say yes because you do not know how to say no? Here and now, I am giving you full permission to "just say no!"

Be honest with yourself. If you are saying yes in order to keep the peace, to avoid guilt, to be liked, to feel needed, or to make others happy, then it is time to come up with strategies for diplomatically saying no. Actually, saying no is akin to doing the right thing because the more times you say yes without really wanting to, the more resentment and anger builds within you. This resentment will come out in other ways and hurt your relationships far more than simply saying no in the first place.

Saying yes to something one normally would not do or does not want to do happens quite often, especially among those who are trying to be accepted and loved. They lose themselves in their relationships, give up their power, and submit to what the other person wants. This can happen in friendships, families, intimate relationships, business partnerships, and student/teacher interactions.

There are lots of benefits to saying no, such as avoiding feeling overwhelmed, stressed, burnt out, scattered, or resentful. This leads to reducing poor quality work, while having more free time, energy, and control. Ultimately, managing requests and saying no when appropriate allow you to live a balanced life.

Whether you are being asked to contribute money, volunteer at an event, or to work late, it is possible to say no in a way that is non-offensive and effective. For example, a friend asks for a monetary contribution for her charity walk. You might say yes in order to avoid offending the person. Or you can say something like, "How wonderful that you're raising money for such a worthwhile cause. Right now it's not in my budget, but I wish you much success in getting donations." You have acknowledged the importance of what the person is working toward, you gave her a reason that is hard to argue with, and you have wished her well. There is not even the word *no* in the response!

The steps to tactfully say no are:

- **Be respectful**—acknowledge what the person is trying to do—raise money, move their furniture, etc. If you have been asked to join a committee or serve in some other way, thank them for considering you—"I'm honored you thought of asking me,"

- **Set boundaries**—do not give all of the reasons why you are unable to fulfill the request. You can simply say something like, "I'm not in a position to do that right now," or "I have a policy not to stray from my budget." In the case above where you are asked to serve in some way, let them know that your schedule will not allow it. No specifics needed.

- **Don't apologize**—You are well within your right to say no. No apology necessary. Stand in your power as you decline the request.

- **Be confident**—Even if all you have planned is a bubble bath, be confident that your relaxation time is just as important as anything someone else wants from you.

- **Stay firm**—If the person pushes—"Oh, come on. Help me out with this." Stick with the reason you gave originally. "My schedule just doesn't allow it."

- **Offer an option**—If you would like to help out, offer another date when you are available or suggest another resource the person might tap into.

Exercise 2-20: Before taking action that someone else wants you to take, consider the pros and cons of what is suggested. Does it feel right to you? Does your body relax or tense up? Do you feel happy and excited at the thought of it, or do you feel sad and reluctant? Say no unless it is an activity for the highest good or that you really want to do. Try the strategies above to help you diplomatically handle turning down requests.

Doing something that is against your core beliefs for the sake of another brings despair. Maybe you just do not want to do it, or you want to spend the time doing something else, even if it is just relaxing. To say no is to exercise free will and maintain sovereignty in your thoughts and actions.

Shift Your Perspective: On Shopping Online

During the holiday season or any busy entertaining time, stress levels increase. The time spent on preparing for the holidays, shopping for gifts and food, cleaning and decorating the house to receive company, on top of your normal, daily responsibilities, tends to diminish the fun of the festivities themselves.

To save yourself some time, shop online. You can buy gifts *and* you can order groceries or catering to be delivered without having to leave the house. You will save aggravation by avoiding the need to fight traffic and can wait for your orders to arrive (even gift wrapped, if you pay a little extra) while you are doing something else, like cleaning the house.

Do your best to enjoy the holidays and other celebrations by minimizing the frustration and pressure that come along with them. You will have a much better time than if you run yourself ragged and receive your guests exhausted and stressed.

Exercise 2-21: Be as kind to yourself as you plan to be toward others during the holidays and at all celebrations, especially those you are managing.

Shift Your Perspective: On Spring Cleaning

Look around you, in your home and/or your business. For many, it is one and the same. Does the energy feel stagnant? Have things been piling up, and you have not had a chance to address the clutter?

The more stuff, dirt, and dust that accumulates in your space, the more you will feel it energetically, resulting in being less motivated and more likely to experience anxiety or depression. Purging your environment of unnecessary items and papers allows the energy to flow through the space. That includes closets!

It is also a lot easier to clean. When tabletops, desktops, and floors are clear of clutter, it is easy to dust and vacuum. It is really amazing how fresh, open, and new your old space can feel when it is clean and clutter-free. You may get really ambitious and give a room or two a new coat of paint.

Exercise 2-22: Select one room or closet. Remove all of the items that no longer serve a purpose or that represent an old way of being. Feel how the energy moves through the space and modify the furniture layout to make the room feel more open. Start from the ceiling, dust around the top of the room, and work your way down to dusting and finally vacuuming. Continue to do this throughout your living and/or workspace as needed.

All of this activity is perfectly aligned with the energies of spring and new beginnings. You will feel refreshed and inspired when you transform your space from cluttered to clear. Top it off with a space cleansing with a sage wand or spray to clear away any stagnant or unwanted energetic remnants. Spring cleaning is an inexpensive way to get an immediate lift in mood and outlook.

Shift Your Perspective: On Starting Over

A DianeWing.com community member wrote to me and said, "I must say I'm growing weary of always walking down a new path. Not that I do not have the strength to carry on and the will to do it, but I really want to feel secure and settled in my life. The fact that I'm constantly searching is starting to overwhelm me. I ask myself 'Why am I always starting over again?'"

She makes an excellent point. Sometimes, it does feel like you are always at the beginning. You start over each time you learn something new because you are viewing life with new eyes and a clearer perspective. It may prompt you to change paths yet again. This is a function of personal evolution. Internal changes prompt external changes. At the same time, it is really a continuation of what came before since lessons and skills acquired on the other paths are likely to be utilized on the new one. Nothing happens on its own; it is always a function of what came before it.

As far as always searching, the quest is what makes life interesting and allows you to explore previously unknown trails that bring new ideas and realizations to light. If security and a sense of feeling settled means that the search is over, then there is less opportunity for evolving over time. Security is a function of feeling solid within the self and having a sense that you are moving forward in accordance with your true nature regardless of the circumstances. To feel settled, the vision of your ideal life must be determined. Once attained, comfort replaces doubt, and satisfaction with where you are in life replaces agitation.

Exercise 2-23: Identify a time when you felt like you were starting from the beginning or when you began walking a new path. What made the change happen? What made you feel the need to begin again on a different road? What did you learn that made you realize that the path you were walking needed to shift? Write down all of the things you learned that brought you to the moment of realization.

Now consider your life vision from the perspective of what would bring the greatest satisfaction. Move through the vision in your mind and see how it feels to live in this way. If it feels joyful, then you are on the right track. If it still feels unsettled, then continue to refine the vision until happiness is most prominent.

No matter how often you begin again, it is never wasted time for all paths lead to the Self. Your journey continues to shift because *you* continue to shift. It took many years to get where you are now, so be patient with yourself as you come out the other side and get clearer with each step. You are where you should be on the path at the perfect time for your growth and development.

Shift Your Perspective: On Success

There are several dictionary definitions of success. Two that are most pertinent to this discussion are "an event that accomplishes its intended purpose" and "a state of prosperity or fame." The first is the definition that is the focus of the work at hand, rather than the second, which focuses on the more common societal view of personal success. It places value on status, money, and projected image.

What do you call success? How are you defining it? When you look at whether or not you have achieved success, consider what you have chosen as your vision. Does your life look like what you have always wanted it to be? If it is lacking, in what specific way does it fall short of your expectations?

Think about the ways in which you measure success. Is it based on someone else's ideal of what you should be doing or your own? If you have achieved someone else's idea of success, you may be experiencing unhappiness, and you probably lack a sense of fulfillment and contentment.

Does success look like a certain amount of money, the level at which you help others, or the amount of creative expression you have?

Society has its standards of what success looks like, and the majority of people strive to attain it despite how unhappy it makes them or how stressed they feel. Climbing the corporate ladder, becoming famous, or achieving a law or medical degree are some examples of what society defines as success. I know many people in corporate jobs who make a lot of money, but who are unhappy in the rigid, stressful, political environment inherent in most large corporations. The same goes for professionals such as doctors and lawyers who find themselves miserable in their work life despite the outward appearance of success. Given that work takes up a large part of the day, this creates significant detriments to achieving happiness. Of course, there are exceptions, and those who remain do it for their own reasons. At the same time, their reasons for pursuing certain vocations may start out differently than they end up when the person discovers that the work does not match his or her true nature.

Depression can result when you fall short of achieving what others want from you. By defining your personal idea of success, you are more likely to feel energized and excited about striving toward what you really want. Success is a very personal endeavor; make it your own! Succeeding by your own standards allows you to function in accordance with your true nature and to experience a level of comfort not otherwise possible. Engaging in work that produces personal growth, healthy relationships, and a way to make a positive impact on the world increases contentment and is the type of success that brings happiness.

How many times have you looked around and felt that others were more successful than you feel you are? Is it the amount of money they make, the large home, or the jet-set lifestyle they lead? Now look at them again. Is it only the material things they have that you want? Or is it a close family, healthy relationships, and a peaceful existence?

Exercise 2-24: Start by writing down a list of the external indicators of success, like money, type of residence you prefer, and how many hours you want to work. Then make a list of the internal indicators of success, such as creative freedom and what type of lifestyle makes you happy. Include everything you can think of on both lists. Focus on what you want, not what you think is possible.

Now look it over while you check in with yourself using my four-part inner guidance system. How does your body feel as you read each item on the list? Does it tense or relax? How do you feel emotionally as you read—exhilarated or stressed? What thoughts come into your mind? Are you flooded with ideas and visions of how to move forward and joy at succeeding, using that particular measure, or are you feeling nervousness at the prospect of having that indicator fulfilled?

Circle the top three to five items combined in both the internal and external success indicator lists that make you feel the best, that light you up, and that feel most like who you are. Take these and write them on a separate piece of paper. Can you imagine feeling successful having these manifest in your life? Does it feel closer to who you are, or does it represent the standards imposed by familial and societal expectations? If the latter, go through the list again, until you can get to the core of what success means on your own terms.

Put it all together to create a solid vision of your happiest, most successful life. For some, it is creating a happy family life and all the things it takes to make that happen. For others, freedom is the most important indicator of success—to have a flexible work schedule, creative expression in their work, and the ability to set their own goals in accordance with their vision.

Trying to fulfill someone else's idea of success leads to a sense of failure and despair because it does not allow for your unique notion of how you want to live your life. When you determine your definition of success and decide the type of life you want to live, then it is easier to see the path to your desires and to set goals along the way.

Shift Your Perspective: On Trees

Feeling ragged around the edges? Your tolerance level at zero? Take a walk in the woods. Trees are amazing beings, capable of clearing toxic energies and rejuvenating the spirit. Connect with them as you walk; feel the anxiety drop away as you are able to take a deep breath. Sense the forest around you, smell its fragrance, listen to the wildlife, and take in the magnificence of mature trees, moss, and fungi. You may even catch a glimpse of a nature spirit or converse with a tree spirit.

Forests have long been fabled transformational sites for heroes and villains alike. They are the epitome of transformation, for the forest is constantly changing. We can take a lesson from deciduous forests through the seasons, watching them go through the budding, blossoming, color-changing, and finally the dropping of leaves. We go through similar cycles of death and rebirth within ourselves. Walking in the forest allows you to connect with the vibration of change and understand that change itself is a constant—it is not good nor bad; it just is. Trees teach us to go with the flow of our own natural cycles and not fight against them.

Being among trees is an important way to ground. Push your aura to reach trees on either side of the path. Mentally ask the trees for permission to connect. With their approval, pull in fresh energy while dumping negative or stale energy into the earth through your feet. With each step, energy blocks are eliminated and replaced with the vital green energy of the trees. The woods encourage the chakras to open wider to accept the life force of the trees. The volume of positive energy flowing in pushes away negativity and allows light to flourish within.

Clearing yourself of negative energies and being in the relaxing environment of the woods gives you a mini-vacation from daily stress.

Exercise 2-25: Dumping Negativity While Walking: As you walk, focus on releasing dense and unwanted energies (emotions, thoughts, experiences, and beliefs). Envision it coming out of your skin and allow it to flow back and away from you. As the unwanted energy releases, you will see a wake of energy in your mind's eye. Be considerate of others and make sure no one is behind you. No one wants to be engulfed in another's energetic waste. Picture the energy coming out of your head, your back, and your legs. As you swing your arms, expel the energy that no longer serves you. Let go of the tension, stress, anger, worry, doubt, and fear as you walk and feel lighter with each movement.

Each time I embark on a woodland journey, I feel my shoulders relax, my breath deepen, and a smile come across my face. My thoughts become clear, inspiration comes, and I am humbled to share the power of the trees. To be surrounded by the forest is the most profound magickal and spiritual experience for me. Find the nearest park or drive to parks farther away to have a new woodland experience.

Trees add beauty and health to any environment. They provide support and shelter for local wildlife, as well as amazing benefits that are not readily apparent. For example, for every 5 percent of tree cover added to a community, storm water runoff is reduced by approximately 2 percent. Trees produce oxygen and conserve energy needed to heat and cool homes and buildings.

Trees are energy boosters as well as toxin cleansers. They take away the denser energies we bring and help raise our vibrational level. Try it for yourself. Next time you are downhearted, take a walk in the woods and feel the lift you receive by the time you leave.

Trees can honor departed loved ones when planted in their names. You can also create your own legacy by planting a tree in your own name. Find trees that are appropriate for your area, and then study the metaphysical properties of the choices. Select a tree based on the energy you wish to bring to that particular area. You can even create a sacred grove on your property or in your neighborhood.

Get together with some of your neighbors and have each contribute a tree or two. There may be local organizations where you can donate a tree to plant for an area in need. Increasing the number of trees is a wonderful way to raise the planet's vibration!

Chapter 3: Regarding the Eternal

Shift Your Perspective: On Control

How many times have you wished that you could make someone do one thing or another—love you, be cooperative, be more ambitious, or believe what you believe... (the list goes on and on)? Or have you wanted to have complete control at work or with your life in general? Or have you wanted to try making something happen more quickly? What was your reaction when it did not happen? Frustration? Anger? Agitation?

Control is the act of exercising authority, managing, or having power over something or someone. This can apply to both internally- and externally-focused targets. Many times, the focus is to exert control over external forces, people, or circumstances. Trying to dominate events goes against Universal Law. The act of allowing things to happen as they are meant to in the time they are supposed to creates a calmer approach to life where acceptance, rather than control, prevails.

Most things in life are out of our direct control. Trying to control external circumstances is by and large out of the scope of what is reasonable. There are too many variables to account for all of them. In attempting to control a circumstance, there is no way to manage every interaction required to create the exact scenario you wish to manifest.

The best and most effective option is to control the self—the thoughts, emotions, and reactions to external stimuli. You have control over the quality of work you produce, the way you treat others, the condition of your living space, and the way you feel on a daily basis. In each moment, you choose your reactions, feelings, and thoughts. You have the ability to gain control over negative automatic thoughts that create and exacerbate anxiety. You determine how you feel about and react to occurrences throughout the day.

> **Exercise 3-1:** Gaining control over the self includes exploring the underlying reasons for what you think and feel at any given moment. If you respond in a way that does not serve you, ask yourself what drives that sort of behavior. Is there a belief about yourself or about the situation that makes you react in one way or another?

The more confidence you have, the more control over the self is possible. If you believe in yourself, there is no need to convince others that you are right or to control their behavior. If you feel content there is no need for others' approval. When you accept yourself, everyone and everything around you aligns with that.

If you are striving for inner peace and harmony in your life, the first thing to give up is the need for control. It creates an imbalance that interferes with the paths of others, with the natural order of things, and with your energy level. It is exhausting to try to control everything around you. By doing so, you control nothing.

Having control over the self is an act of ultimate strength and power. Many aspects of a situation may be unknown to any one person, and to admit that much is not known can result in a healthy outlook and minimal need for control.

Accept things as they are, and allow people and circumstances to run their natural course. Have faith in the way things are, and seek to discover the lessons reflected back to you.

By giving up control, things turn out for the best in their own time. Flowing with the energetic tides allows more time for work on the self rather than trying to control what is the Universe's domain.

Shift Your Perspective: On Healing

There are many sources of pain and opportunities to heal—from understanding childhood issues to pain caused in adulthood—it is the memory of the experience that lingers and persists in creating an emotional response that is as powerful as when it originally took place. The pain that began as emotional can sometimes turn into physical, mental, or spiritual illness the longer you hold on to it.

While the actual experience cannot be changed, your reaction to it and your understanding of it can be. No matter when it occurred, viewing it from an objective perspective enables you to see how it affected your life and altered your beliefs and view of yourself.

The wound's depth will determine how long it takes to heal. Be patient with and kind to yourself. Healing is a process, and there is no magic bullet that will obliterate the hurt you feel. Sometimes it requires professional assistance to move forward; other times, the best option is solitary soul searching.

Exercise 3-2: The first step is to get clear on the way the experience hurt you. How has the pain manifested in your life? If you were abandoned, do you feel the need to possess? If you were physically or emotionally harmed, do you avoid close relationships or have intimacy issues? If you were betrayed, do you have a global lack of trust?

Bring kind, non-judgmental, supportive people into your life, and focus on developing healthy, loving relationships. Get the help you need and enhance healing by appropriately directing trust and love toward yourself and others.

To heal completely, each layer of the pain must be addressed—physical, mental, emotional, and spiritual. If the pain originates as a physical illness, search the other three layers to see how they may be contributing to the condition. How do your emotions exacerbate the physical pain? What thoughts come forward regarding your illness and your self-concept as a result of the physical anomaly? What is your spiritual perspective on this? That is, do you feel alone in your healing, or can you connect to the divine for support in healing? If the pain originates in your thoughts/mental layer, go through the same process with the other three layers and how their involvement exacerbates or alleviates your pain. And so on for the emotional and spiritual layer.

Wounds are opportunities to learn and grow. They present challenges to overcome while strengthening you in the process. Without difficulty, you cannot come fully into your power. Use the healing process as a way to explore your true nature and to cultivate resilience in the face of adversity.

Shift Your Perspective: On Imagination

The ability to use imagination has led to great discoveries in science, the creation of amazing literature, and a way to take a break from the objective reality we face each day. The way in which we use the gift of imagination can range from decorating a room in your mind and then taking action to find the pieces that will replicate that mental design to a star athlete practicing his craft in his mind to improve his performance significantly.

In the mind's eye of imagination, we can see things that are not yet in existence and can escape from the discomfort of the present. At its best, the imagination can help us take a mini-vacation and come out feeling refreshed. At its worst, the imagination can be a deadly enemy when it is used to conceive of terrible possibilities that create doubt, fear, and worry.

Your imagination is a powerful tool that can be used to test things (ways of being, a new vocation, a change in relationship) and work out problems, or it can keep you stuck in a self-made realm of disappointment. For example, if you are in the habit of imagining certain outcomes that never quite meet your expectations, you set yourself up for disappointment. Or if you continually focus on worrying about what could happen and feeling the need to prepare for it, you are heading for continuous anxiety.

> **Exercise 3-3:** When you catch yourself imagining unhealthy or upsetting scenarios, recognize that you have the power to make a mental shift to convert them into anything you want, something pleasant and uplifting, to alleviate tension and even put a smile on your face.

When you use your imagination creatively and in positive ways, you will transform your energy into a higher vibrational frequency and start attracting more positive people and situations to your life. In this way, you step into an expansive realm of possibilities.

Shift Your Perspective: On Intention

Intention is the primary tool we use to shape our lives. With each gesture, thought, intention, action, and interaction, we move energy.

For many, the word "intention" brings forth the idea of an affirmation, saying what you want over and over again in hopes that it comes true or until you start to believe it. I call this *wishcraft* and feel that while this is one way to begin the journey of goal-setting, there are more powerful methods for claiming intention. In its formal definition, intention is an anticipated outcome that guides your actions.

There must be clear intent before energy can be moved in a specific direction. The desire and motivation of the originator directs the flow and texture of the energy. What manifests is dictated by intention. Intention is the key to focusing your attention and, thereby, directing the energy.

Energy is directed by determining a specific goal and visualizing the attainment of that goal. The moving of the energy is what is important— the ability to direct the energy to manifest what intention and will dictates. Be clear on your motivation and intent in your interactions and in formulating your desires. If you do not know what you want, you cannot direct your energy toward it. Making the choice, understanding why you are choosing it, and tapping into the motivation behind it serves to direct energy, behavior, and actions in a laser-focused way. The accumulation and specific release of energy is the key to manifestation of a vision.

It is important to identify your intention before proceeding with any plan of action. The intention defines the outcome you strive to create. It requires looking deep into the request you are making to the Universe and asking why you want it and how your life will be different once you have it.

Every thought, feeling, belief, and action draws certain types of energy to you. The key is to be intentional with the type of energy you are pulling toward you. It is about being mindful of what your underlying motivation is. One action can hold within it a variety of intentions that are compelled by certain motivations.

For example, the action is that a person helps out at an event. The motivation could be 1) to make it a truly wonderful experience for all, 2) to be around people and have a social outlet, 3) to show off a skill or talent, or 4) to network with others. The intention may be 1) to get accolades for your work, 2) to show others that you are superior in your skill set, 3) to do a good deed that will benefit many, or 4) to increase business opportunities. The energy of each of these is very different from one another and dictates the way the action is approached. So before undertaking any activity or plan, ask yourself, "What is my intention?"

The intention may be to help or to harm, to attract or to repel, to gain or to lose. Whichever the choice, the underlying intention modifies behavior and activity around the circumstance.

Exercise 3-4: If you are finding that things are not going as planned, take a step back and go deep into yourself to discover the true motivation and underlying intention. It may not be what you thought it was on the surface. When determining a goal, take time to write down what the real motivation is behind your desire to get crystal clear on your intention. Additionally, before entering into an interpersonal interaction, consider what your intention is during the conversation. Is it to persuade or influence? To admonish or criticize? To uplift and inspire? Clarify your intention and modify accordingly; then align your words and approach with your intention to achieve the best result.

Another example: You have dreamed of owning a home. Why? The act of buying a home may have the intention of creating security and space for you and your family, or to impress others, or to have an investment. The type and location of the home will be determined by your ultimate intention.

If you set an intention to create peace and harmony in your life, then your actions will be directed accordingly, and the Universe will respond in kind. If your intention is of a low vibration, then that is what will come into your life. There are those whose intention is to deceive, and their behavior follows suit.

When you around those who harbor negative intent, the projected energy can be highly detrimental. Being around those who have kind thoughts and intentions uplifts the vibrational frequency rather than diminishing it. Which do you choose to project?

Shift Your Perspective: On Letting Go

You have heard it before—Just Let It Go... and everything will be okay. But what if you cannot let it go? What if the despair, anger, and discord toward a person or situation continues to mount?

Many people struggle with this issue on a regular basis. They have been in relationships with family members or a romantic partner who turned out to be different from what they thought. A lover finds someone new; a family situation is unfair. Whether it is family or a lover, when things go bad, the sense of betrayal can be palpable. When you continue to focus on it, seethe over it, or renew the anger day by day by playing the scenario over and over again in your mind, it does not do anything to remedy the way you are feeling.

In fact, it makes it worse. In extreme cases, holding on to the anger and betrayal leads to severe insomnia or even self-destructive behavior. It leads to the inability to perform at work, and it inhibits healthy relationships with others who have nothing to do with the relationship that is causing the problem.

The most immediate strategy is to stop playing the scenario over and over again in your mind, trying to find reasons why it happened. Wanting closure in the form of finding out why someone acts the way he or she does or treated you one way or another is understandable, but not always possible. This is a situation that is out of your control, and it is completely up to the other person or people to offer explanations that may or may not come, so let us remove this from the list of possible solutions.

These things happen for the same reason anything else in our lives happens: to teach us lessons we are here to learn.

> **Exercise 3-5:** Remove the anger, the hatred, the guilt, the sadness—basically, get rid of the drama—and take a look at it from an objective viewpoint. What is held within the situation that shows you an aspect of yourself that needs to be worked on? How can understanding the situation make your life better in the long run?

For example, if a long-term romantic relationship goes bad and the other person rejects you for someone else, what lesson is here? Is it that they needed space? Is the situation reflecting the lesson of freedom versus control? Constantly saying to yourself that you did nothing wrong and that the situation is unfair is not going to help you move past the circumstance and see the lesson. Step back. What happened between you may not be right or wrong; it just may be that your energies were no longer aligned. Could it be time to find yourself outside the context of another person?

So when you are fuming at someone who has hurt you, take a moment to ground yourself and ask the Universe, "What is the lesson I need to get from this experience?"

Shift Your Perspective: On Love

The romanticized version of love is what causes much pain in relationships. The idea of what poets and movies tell you love should look like is unrealistic for most people. There are definite rewards each person gets from the other, roles each plays in the relationship, and expectations of the other that may or may not be fulfilled.

Your definition of love guides and attracts your relationships. Whether you have healthy, loving relationships or dysfunctional, difficult ones, it all ties back to your definition of love. Most people learn what love is from the parental interaction. At a young age, parents teach what is expected from you, what you can expect from them, and the nature of that relationship. It also colors the relationship you have with yourself and your capacity for self-love.

During personal and client interactions, I have noticed patterns in those who are struggling in relationships of all types—intimate, work, friends, and family. They all have a similar sense to them, a clear pattern that repeats itself in all aspects of life. And then it jumped out at me; their definition of love sets the tone for all of their relationships and the types of relationships they attract.

When the word love is mentioned, the mind goes to the emotional response and connotation. While love can bring the most exuberant joy, it can also result in incredible sorrow. It has been the reason for great acts of selflessness, as well as horrific atrocities.

Everybody wants love, to be loved, to give love. Love provides a sense of connection, of self-worth, and belonging. Some people go through many relationships, trying to find the one where they feel safe and secure. Others endure terrible treatment by those they believe do it out of love or because they fear no one else will love them.

Love in its purest form carries a high vibrational frequency. It incorporates compassion and kindness toward others and allows an expression of love to extend out into the world through care and support. At the other end of the love continuum, the journey is difficult and fraught with darkness. Understanding the shadow side of love is critical in order to transcend that negativity and to manifest love in its most beautiful expressions.

To get to the heart of what is needed in a relationship is to have a clearer picture of what to look for in a partner. The first experience people have with love is the parental or caregiver interaction and how it is experienced. The phrase "You married your mother/father" has a lot of truth to it since the relationship you experienced with one or the other parent is in the cellular memory as familiar. Some may feel that difficult parental interactions have been buried or put aside, but in most cases, the effects linger into adulthood and show up in all relationships.

Relationships go beyond physical attraction, the chemistry everyone is looking for, and allow the initial passion to mature into a deep and satisfying love. What follows is a reduction in arguments and a faster resolution when there is a tiff. Even if there is an initial attraction, if the person falls short in daily interactions, the physical attraction wears off, whereas with a genuine liking and caring for each other, desire to be with the other person continues.

Healthy relationships have less struggle and drama and more fun and peace. If a relationship is hard—if you have to put in a monumental effort every day or if the same issues keep coming up despite repeated discussion—then it is time to reconsider the definition of love being used. If every day is an effort, then you are with the wrong person. Yes, it takes patience, understanding, and a willingness to overlook annoying habits of the other person, but seeing the big relationship picture is more important. The relationship needs to display a healthy overall pattern in order to tolerate the other stuff. Acceptance of one another is key.

Attracting and creating a healthy relationship with the right partner is based in how love is defined. The type of relationship that exists is the one that the individual is ready for. Very few relationships seem to satisfy the need for fulfillment because of striving for the romantic ideal and being sorely disappointed. Instead of this approach, the definition of love comes from early parental/caregiver interactions that set the tone for all other relationships—in work, with friends, with family members, and with lovers.

> **Exercise 3-6:** Define love. What does love mean to you? How do you want to feel in the ideal relationship? Does your definition support healthy relationships and sense of intimacy? What specific behaviors are included when you think of loving gestures—both giving and receiving?

Shift Your Perspective: On Patience

One of my community members wrote to me and said, "I am not a patient person and having to wait for things to happen/unfold at the right time in my life is a struggle for me. It is very difficult for me just to sit back, wait, be patient, and trust that things will work out the way they are supposed to. Maybe I try to control too many things."

You may feel the same way. Consider the balance of waiting versus taking action. Yes, things happen in their own time, so acceptance and trust are important. While you wait, you can do something that can get you closer to the goal, or you can try out something new to see whether there is value in it. This helps to move things along or may even help you discover that what you thought you wanted is not what you want any longer.

Sometimes, a block is beneficial, for it requires you to contemplate the next move, gather more information, or get additional experience.

> **Exercise 3-7:** Practice shedding any resistance. Dump the worry into the earth and then ground each day before going to sleep. This will even out your energy and allow you to stay focused in the present.

Shift Your Perspective: On Peace

There are three keys to experiencing peace: perspective, acceptance, and gratitude. Many people experience dissatisfaction with their lives. They are remorseful, depressed, and uncertain. Some wish for how it "used to be," others lack a clear vision of what they want their lives to look like. They run into obstacles and blocks that cause them to feel bewildered. There are three keys to overcoming the patterns that keep you stuck.

Exercise 3-8: First, stop complaining. Let go of the anger, sadness, doubt, or other negative emotion that keeps you stuck. Accept where you are in this moment as being the perfect place.

Second, be grateful for everything in your life, whether you consider it to be good or bad. Shift your perspective to consider all circumstances as neutral, a lesson to be learned, or an opportunity for growth.

Third, understand that pessimism, doubt, worry, lack of enthusiasm, and low energy attract relationships and circumstances that reflect those states of being. What you attract is based on how you are on the inside, not what you say you want.

If you are truly ready to experience a peaceful and contented life, it is essential that you shift the way you view yourself and your surroundings. Make this your mantra: Let go. Be grateful. Stay open. See the magick.

Creating a personal sanctuary of peace helps you tolerate the hustle and bustle of everyday life. It is important to have a special place to retreat, a quiet place with clear energy. I recommend selecting a place that is protected from the elements so you can use it regardless of the weather. It can be as big or as small as you like or as your circumstances dictate. The size of the space is not as important as the type of energy you create there. The goal is to feel an instant sense of peace, safety, and serenity upon entering.

The walls or other type of boundary outlining the space is one layer; the energetic boundary you draw is the next. Establish the boundary by sitting in the middle of the space and beam out white light from within yourself and out to each natural edge. Fill the space with your intention of tranquility and harmony. Select an incense or aromatherapy fragrance that makes you feel light and peaceful. Use it exclusively in the space as long as it has a calming effect.

Engage only in tranquil activities while in the space—read, meditate, embroider, draw—whatever helps you decompress and center. If possible, maintain this space for yourself; do not allow others to enter your sacred space. Keep the energy there purely yours. If this is not possible, you can cast the energy each time, say in a bedroom or large closet (if you do not mind your clothes smelling like incense).

In the craziness of life, it is important to carve out a sacred space; one that you can escape to in a moment's notice to relax, recharge, and restore yourself. This haven can be created indoors or outdoors, or it can even be a place created within yourself. When establishing your sacred space, smudge with sage and/or herbs of your choice and set the boundary and intention of the space. If indoors, trace the perimeter of the room or section of the room with your finger while focusing on the intention that this will be your special place for peace and quiet. Send love into every corner of the space and focus on feeling comfortable and centered when you enter. Decorate it with items that make you feel good. You can do this at work or at home. Designate the border with intention. Outdoors you can do the same thing. Choose a grove or corner of your garden. You can even designate a special place in a public park and infuse it with your energy.

When you cannot escape to a physical location, build the sanctuary in your mind. Close your eyes and envision the most idyllic place you can dream of. It can be as big or as small as you like. It can be a magickal forest, a fantastical castle, or a cozy cabin. Build it and channel positive energy into it. Go to this place when you feel overwhelmed or agitated. Enter with reverence for the sacred place that it is. Feel a sense of peace wash over you.

Shift Your Perspective: On Power

Power has been abused for centuries. The idea of power is associated with fame, fortune, controlling others, or having unlimited resources with which to do your bidding. This type of power comes from external sources and the ability to influence that which is outside of oneself. Improper use of power has caused misery, death, and destruction.

Those who do not have access to great financial means and powerful allies often feel weak and unable to take charge of what is going on around them. In this context, the way power is viewed serves to diminish self-worth and perceived control. The result is anxiety, depression, and a sense of helplessness.

> **Exercise 3-9:** How do you define power? What is it you seek to have power over? Do you seek to have power over others or over yourself? Is power external control or influence or something that is used to control oneself?

True power comes from within. It utilizes the internal resources available to all of us: imagination, will, desire, creativity, and intuition. These allow us to control our thoughts and actions. You have the power to choose your path, to select those who walk the path with you, and the purposeful actions you take to express your gifts. You have the power to give up if things get too hard, or to push past obstacles that are in the way of your happiness, health, success, and inner peace. In this sense, power is choice.

You have the power to make someone feel terrible or really wonderful. You have the power to make the world a better place, starting with cleaning up yourself and your immediate environment. You have power over your thoughts rather than allowing them to control you.

In all of these scenarios, responsibility is placed squarely on our shoulders to take control, to learn what is necessary to move forward, to become aware of our gifts and our purpose, and to know how to use our gifts in high service to others.

The power to help another person is the greatest power of all. The most effective and powerful spiritual leaders—Gandhi, Mother Teresa, Jesus, Buddha—did not seek control over others, but they were in high service, and in that way, they became powerful forces of influence for the greater good. The help you put forward need not be on the scale of those just mentioned, but our power is just as great to make a difference in the lives of those around us.

Every time you say you cannot do something or when you act because someone else thinks you should, you give away your power. Each time you succumb to old habits because it is easier than shifting into a new, more effective way of being, your power is diminished. By empowering yourself, acknowledging your value, and using your strength to nurture yourself and others, you wield the greatest power of all.

There is even power in being friendly and courteous. There is a school of thought that power comes from ruling with an iron fist, controlling everything and everyone, and demanding that others follow. This way of being is far from powerful; it is actually a fear-based response to the world. The fear of being out of control, the fear of being left behind as others grow and create, the fear of not mattering in the world.

Instead, power comes from being in high service to others, in being friendly, and in demonstrating courtesy. This creates willing followers who appreciate the help that has been given. The person who leads with courteous, friendly, and helpful behavior is the one others value.

Consider a situation where traffic is heavy and there is a person waiting to pull out of a parking lot and into the lane. You have the power to make that person's day a little easier or more difficult. Most people do not allow the car to pull out in front of them. Notice what happens when you wave the person forward. In the majority of cases, he will gratefully wave and mouth "Thank you." While he does not know you and you do not know him, you have paid forward a kindness that may change that person's day for the better, and it certainly elevates your vibrational level. Kindness triggers kindness, and the next time you are the one waiting to pull into traffic, someone will let you pass.

Courtesy seems to be a lost art form. Whether on the beach or while driving, odds are you have run into the discourteous person who seemingly has no awareness of how his or her actions affect others. Stories of this type of behavior are rampant. You probably have a tale to tell regarding being slighted by a rude person or people.

One person told me about a time when she was sitting on the beach with a friend to watch the sun set. The beach was empty except for the two of them. Another couple came and spread their blanket directly in front of them, blocking their view of the sunset. Despite talking loudly enough for the offending couple to hear regarding their view of being blocked, the interlopers ignored them and stayed right where they were. With an entire beach from which to select a spot, they chose to sit directly in front of someone else's view. They used their power to diminish the experience of others.

The energy this creates is agitated, resentful, and rude. What you create comes back to you. When similar situations manifest in the lives of those who are ignorant, they cannot imagine why and complain about those who behave similarly to how they themselves interact with others. When experiencing a series of rude interactions, it is time to take stock of what these experiences may be reflecting back.

Consider how what you do affects others, for two major reasons: first, we are all connected, so if one person does something to cause discontent for another, it brings down the vibration of the entire energy field. Even something as simple as not paying attention when you are first at a traffic signal can delay all of the people behind you. Be considerate, use common courtesy, and think of how it affects you when others act selfishly or with total disregard of others. Second, whatever you put out comes back to you, so if you create discord and hurtful situations for others, it will come back to you in every aspect of your life.

> **Exercise 3-10:** Take notice of how your actions affect those around you on a regular basis. What you put out comes back to you. While this tip is mentioned above, it is worth mentioning again, as it is a critical concept for your success and happiness. By helping others, giving of yourself, and providing people with a positive experience, you improve your chances of receiving the support you need from the Universe and from others to achieve your desires.

The energy you put out comes back similarly from places you do not expect. Let us say you do a good deed for Harry. The energetic reward will not necessary come back to you directly from Harry, but it may come in the form of help and support from another source when you need it most. If you are hurtful to someone, the negative backlash may not come back to you directly from that person, but it could manifest in the form of another important relationship being compromised or the loss of something important to you. Choose to act in the highest good of yourself and others to raise the vibration of those around you and the planet in general, not just because of the karmic boomerang effect. Keep in mind the direct energetic cause and effect, giving you more power over living an uplifting life.

> **Exercise 3-11:** Next time you help someone, notice how quickly the Universe reciprocates, what form it takes, and from whence the reward comes. Next time you do something that hurts another, notice how quickly the karmic backlash manifests, what form it takes, and how it relates to your negative action.

These two simple exercises can make all the difference in how life is experienced. Being mindful of others and using a friendly, courteous approach builds personal power for the highest good. The power to offer friendly assistance and be courteous is available to you every minute of every day. Being remembered for kindness and high service to others creates the high and very powerful vibration of gratitude, which extends to all aspects of life.

Shift Your Perspective: On Relaxation

Sometimes, you just need a break—from your daily routine, from familiar environments, from your thoughts, and even from yourself. Doing it without feeling guilty or lazy is the key.

One of the best ways to do that is to break away from the norm and experience something new. It can be something simple like taking a walk in a park you have never been to or taking a different way home. It can be about shutting off your mind for a bit and taking a break from the constant chatter. It can be drastic like touring Europe for several weeks. It can be something in between like a relaxing week-long cruise.

Whatever you decide, remember that it is important to incorporate relaxation into your schedule. In our workaholic society, it is so easy to forget that we need to take some time for ourselves, step back, and rejuvenate. In a relaxed state, our minds can conjure amazing ideas that would not have had a voice in the din of the ceaseless stream of thoughts. This is what meditation is about, and it is akin to taking a mini-vacation, but on a grander scale; it is important to change your physical surroundings as well. The break will allow your true self to emerge and enjoy itself.

My relaxing mini-vacations happen in my garden. Working in it clears my head, grounds me, and reconnects me to nature. The sound of the creek, the birds chirping, and being surrounded by lush green plants and trees is the most relaxing environment for me. New story and book ideas flood into my mind as I work with the plants. It also puts me in a meditative state that enhances an overall sense of wellbeing.

It is possible to experience spirituality and calming energies in the most mundane tasks. There is no need to schedule a special time to practice formal meditation when it is easy to incorporate it into everyday undertakings. A garden is a great place to tap into the Universe and connect with yourself.

If this sounds like something you would enjoy, here is my garden meditation technique.

Exercise 3-12: Garden Meditation

Select one particular garden task (deadheading roses, pulling weeds in one section of the garden, etc.). Focus your attention entirely on what you are doing. For example, if deadheading roses, clear your mind and simply focus on finding the expended buds to clip. As you clip, see only the clippers and the bud. If weeding, focus only on pulling the weed and not the plants around it.

Allow the scents, sounds, and sights to wash over you. If a thought comes through, allow it, and then refocus on your task. When I pull weeds, childhood memories of happily helping my grandmother in the garden come gently in. I experience the joy of remembering and then refocus.

As you work, allow the plant to give you insights about yourself and life in general. A weed that grows similar to a vine, reminds me that an issue in one part of life can be linked to issues in other parts of life. By removing it, the other plants seem to breathe easier around it, the problem gone, just as when we address problems that impact our lives and we can take a deep breath of relief.

See what insights come through and then refocus on your task. By the time you are finished, you will feel wonderful and your garden chores will be complete without it feeling like work! You can do the same with any task you choose, even mopping the floor.

Shift Your Perspective: On Sacrifice

I have heard people say things like "I sacrificed everything for him!" or "What do I have to sacrifice to make things right?"

This idea of having to sacrifice something for someone or to a deity of some sort, such as promising the Universe that you will give up something if It provides the thing you desire, has been around as long as humankind has walked the earth. Yet the idea of sacrifice has been muddied—in the actions of cultures that sacrificed animals and humans to a deity to convince the god to do what they needed and by those people who felt that self-sacrifice was a way to manipulate someone to get them to do what they wanted. It creates scenarios ripe to foster resentment and disappointment.

In addition to the above definitions of sacrifice, it is also considered to mean "The act of losing or surrendering something as a penalty for a mistake or fault or failure to perform, etc." and "[something] surrendered or lost in order to gain an objective." [WordWeb]

With all of these scenarios, the act of sacrifice indicates a giving up of something to get something else. In a different context, the idea of sacrifice is more closely aligned to the idea that shedding old ways of being and killing off old beliefs and, therefore, the old Self are the sacrifices required for growth. This is not to say that what is a valued aspect of self should be removed, but rather, it is something that must be released in order to transform. This released energy creates room for the new, the fresh, and the higher vibrational types of energies that are aligned to who you are now and who you are trying to become.

Old energies and beliefs cloud the psyche and prevent clear vision of your ideal existence. The more you hold on to the hurt feelings, disappointments, and other negative types of memories, the less likely you are to see past them and get on with your life in more positive ways. Sacrifice these outmoded ways of being and you will feel renewed, refreshed, and ready to shed the relationships, emotions, behaviors, and beliefs that are holding you back.

It is not about sacrificing the Self in the sense of saving another, but rather allowing the death of a part of the self that is no longer appropriate to your path in order to save the Self—whether it is a personality trait or an external behavior, habit, or belief. Death of an old way of being is the only way to transform and create a new beginning.

Exercise 3-13: Choose an aspect of yourself to sacrifice: beliefs, behaviors, habits, or ways of being. Picture a stone altar in your mind. Decorate it however you would like. Now give the aspect which you are sacrificing a physical form. It may be a habit like smoking, so imagine it as a pack of cigarettes with your picture on it. Place it on the altar and choose a way to obliterate it, such as setting it on fire and watching it burn to ash. Make the images crystallize in your mind, and feel the shift as the habit is destroyed before you. Do this whenever you are ready to *sacrifice* the next aspect of the Self that no longer serves you.

Shift Your Perspective: On Silence

We are bombarded every day with noise—trucks and cars going by, lawn mowers, sirens, television, and people chattering. On some level, we have grown used to having a constant stream of sound around us without realizing the negative effect it has on our ability to process information cognitively and to express our creativity. Noise and silence have different and significant results on the energy around us and within us.

Studies suggest that road and air traffic noise also have an adverse impact on blood pressure. People who live in consistently loud environments experience elevated levels of stress hormones. Anxiety may also increase depending on whether or not we have control over the noise's source. Noise can cause us to be distracted when trying to complete a task, result in an inability to relax or sleep, and even hurt creativity due to the disruption of abstract processing. Certain sounds may promote relaxation or creativity, such as music or the sounds of nature, yet a study by Luciano

Bernardi in 2006 showed that two-minute stretches of silence were even more relaxing.

Depending on your unique disposition, the introduction of sound may feel necessary when alone to soothe feelings of loneliness. Those who dislike being alone tend to have the radio or television on the majority of the time. Then there are the empaths, who are sensitive to the energies of others, as well as to noise and sound in general, and who seek quiet environments as a result. Whichever group we place ourselves in, the effects of continuous exposure to noise and sound may not be readily apparent until we have the opportunity to experience utter silence.

In a study by Michael Wehr (2010), it was discovered that our brains stop reacting when there is continuous sound, and the change to silence triggers a separate network of neurons. A study by Imke Kirste (2013) discovered that two hours of silence per day encouraged cell development in the hippocampus, the region of the brain related to the formation of memory.

Interestingly, in the face of silence, the brain will create its own internal sounds, such as when we are able to hear a song in our heads that is not playing externally within the environment. At the same time, freedom from noise and tasks allows us to process the information we are exposed to on a regular basis. Being in a quiet place allows us to know ourselves better. It gives us the opportunity to be with ourselves and to have a deep discussion with ourselves about what we think and feel. While noise distracts us from thoughts and feelings we may find upsetting or disturbing, it does not allow us to understand that distress and to deal with it at a core level.

The need for silence has popularized sensory deprivation tanks: a soundproof, lightproof, salt-water filled tank that isolates the person from sensory input and allows one to float on top of the water to experience a sense of weightlessness. This environment allows a heightened sense of introspection for most, and hallucinations and out-of-body experiences for some. Spiritual retreats that focus on quiet meditative activities also seek to produce a deep sense of relaxation and connection to self and spirit.

Wooded places with little to no human population provide the perfect environment to commune with oneself. On a trip to the Shenandoah Valley in Virginia, my husband and I hiked a few miles down a snow-covered trail and came to rest on some logs in a place where there was absolute silence. Not a bird chirped nor deer scampered. It was one of the most profound experiences with silence I have had. (The other was in the crypt at Canterbury Cathedral in Canterbury, England.) We sat for a long while, not talking, just experiencing. My whole body relaxed, a sense of joy and peace washed over me, and I reveled in the deep quiet that is all too rare in daily life.

Now that we have an increased awareness of the role noise and sound play in our daily lives and the ways in which silence can enhance our cognitive function, overall performance, and health, it is time to test this concept. By noticing our stress level when around noise versus silence, we can distinguish the benefits of a noise-free environment and the difference in energy from one condition to the other. How much noise is in the environment? How much do we have control over (television, for example), and how much is out of our control (sounds of road and air traffic)?

Exercise 3-14: Try eliminating sound when alone. Turn off the television, stereo, or radio. The ability to hear thoughts and internal dialogue will increase. Assess the level of concentration that can be achieved in a quiet environment. Determine the stress level in the body. Cultivate peace and heighten concentration and creativity by reducing or eliminating the amount of noise experienced on a regular basis. Try it and see how the energy shifts for the better.

Shift Your Perspective: On Spirituality

Perspective is reality, and what you believe drives your behavior and the way you feel about life. This includes spiritual practice. If you feel scattered, jumping from one modality to the next, one guru to the next, it is time to sit down and get to the heart of what you believe in order to define spirituality for yourself.

Each person has a unique view and way of responding to spiritual beliefs and practices. Even when groups form based on a primary belief system, such as with Christianity, Paganism, New Age, or Buddhism, there are many variations on these systems and the way they approach life and spiritual practice.

Some groups take a more eclectic approach, combining the aspects of each system they feel rings true.

Exercise 3-15: Consider the goals you are trying to achieve through your chosen practice and beliefs. Are you focused on methods to connect to Spirit in a more consistent and meaningful way? If so, how do you define the idea of Spirit? This definition determines whether your current approach is the most effective way for you to interact with Spirit.

Is your approach monotheistic (one God or overarching energy) or polytheistic (many gods)? Do you prefer a strict, organized approach, or a more free-flowing one? Do you enjoy participating in spiritual practice with groups, as an individual, or a combination of both?

Journal about your experiences. Have you been performing certain spiritual practices out of habit? Do they still serve you given your current level of understanding? Is your spirituality inherited, that is, adopted from family traditions? If so, what does it mean for you?

After defining Spirit and spiritual beliefs for yourself, ask: How does your definition of spirituality change your perception of the world and how you choose to behave? Are you embodying your beliefs and the nature of Spirit as you have defined it? What needs to change in order to be aligned with this mindset and belief system?

All paths are valid. When the path you choose aligns with your true nature, it will bring you the most satisfaction, fulfillment, and profound connection to the Universe.

Shift Your Perspective: On Strength

When you think of strength, what comes to mind? Is it physical strength to lift and carry groceries, your child, or some other item? Is it emotional strength to get through the day and to withstand stress and drama? Do you associate strength with mental agility, clarity, development of a personal will, and fortitude of purpose? Or is it the strength that comes from connecting to Spirit for guidance and support?

Actually, it is all of the above. Depending on the situation at hand, each becomes essential, both individually and collectively, for successfully navigating daily life and long-term goals. Building strength physically, emotionally, mentally, and spiritually allows you to withstand turmoil and be more resilient in the face of change.

Developing strength in all of these areas makes it easier to call upon it when needed and provides the ability to transition gracefully from one challenge or opportunity to the next. Whether you desire to help those in transition and provide nurturing support or whether you are attempting to protect yourself against negative energies, strength is required. At the same time, using your strength to fight against change creates discomfort, anxiety, and fatigue for yourself and those around you.

Strength comes from within you, built within your energy bodies. In the physical body, it is important to eat a healthy, nutritious diet and to exercise. Building up your physical body provides a solid foundation for you to build strength in the other energy bodies. An unhealthy body can create dis-ease in not only the physical, but also in the mental and emotional. It is true that your "body is a temple" (1 Corinthians 6:19-20) and without a strong, healthy body, it can be difficult to think clearly, feel emotionally stable, or connect to Spirit.

Strength comes from Spirit. As you accept Spirit into your "temple," you become stronger as a result of the inner peace and harmony that Spirit provides. Stress is reduced and joy is increased when you reach the understanding that all decisions need not be made on your own; you have Divine Will to guide you.

Strength comes from your subconscious mind as it reaches your conscious mind. You develop a strong will with which to move forward, bolster your resolve, and increase self-confidence. Strength is achieved through clear thinking, increased self-awareness, and applied wisdom. It allows self-trust to follow inner guidance, promotes confidence in your abilities to achieve your goals, and encourages you to take action.

Emotional strength comes as a result of letting go of the past, releasing the poor-me mentality, erasing the tendency to find fault and blame others, and increasing the ability to embrace joyful visions of your ideal life.

Exercise 3-16: Explore the reasons you hold on to negative emotions like anger, fear, depression, and anxiety. Seek to replace them with joy, excitement, and faith. Take responsibility for what your life looks like. Start your day with a positive statement such as "I find joy in all I do," or "I am grateful for all that is in my life." Whether you believe it or not, say it anyway. It will get your neural network shifting into new patterns. Say it every day for twenty-eight days. That is the minimum amount of time it takes to create a new habit. Watch the amazing changes the world makes as you create this new way of feeling about yourself and your life.

Determine which "body" you need to work on the most—physical, mental, emotional, or spiritual. Take action to open yourself to a new way of being that supports your dreams and desires. Develop focus and concentrate on what you want. Embody the strength it takes to manifest it in your life.

You have the power and the strength waiting within you. It is up to you to develop and utilize it for your highest good.

Shift Your Perspective: On Transformation

Transformation is a buzzword used to discuss the change we can expect from using a certain product, technique, modality, or from a way of being or thinking. Change is sought during times of discomfort, frustration, confusion, or anxiety. The desired change may be physical, emotional, mental, or spiritual.

In the sense of physical transformation, transformation may apply to diet, exercise, or appearance to improve health, lose weight, or be more appealing. In the case of emotions, it may be that we want to let go of painful or toxic emotions such as grief, fear, anxiety, anger, or depression to attain an elevated mood and vibrational frequency. Mental transformation may take on the work of stopping and challenging negative automatic thoughts about ourselves or the world in order to move forward confidently and to avoid self-sabotage. For spiritual transformation, it means embodying the essence of the divine and trusting the guidance received from the Universe.

Transformation implies a qualitative change, as in the quality of life, and it is achieved by way of focused attention and mindfulness. First is to determine what the end result looks like. If there is uncertainty in this regard, the odds of success are diminished. Envision yourself as you want to look, if the desired transformation is physical. If emotional, picture the joy, peace, or whatever type of mood is wanted. If mental, imagine gliding through the day on a wave of positive thoughts. If spiritual, sense the higher, lighter vibration of connection to Spirit.

In addition, be clear on how the hoped-for transformation affects each level of being, on every plane of existence. Deep, lasting change occurs on every level, so getting clear on how that would materialize allows for a quicker, more complete shift.

Let us take losing weight, for example. On the surface, it seems to be a physical transformation, yet the other levels of being must also undergo a shift in order for the desired physical change to occur. Many times, excess weight is the result of fear and worry, so the extra pounds serve to protect and shield. Addressing this level requires the fear to be eliminated. Now the mental layer. What thoughts go along with weight gain? Not being good enough? Thinking that no amount of effort will take off the weight? Finally, does it seem like no support is available? Connection to the divine brings a sense of partnership and assistance that going it alone does not provide.

The best way to identify the needed transformation and know whether you are on the right track is to use your four-part inner guidance system that tells you when you are making decisions in alignment with your highest good.

Start by checking in with your body's reactions. When you experience something, does your body tense up or relax? If tense, is it in your shoulders (carrying responsibility for what happened), your chest (having an emotional reaction to what happened), or your stomach (having a fear reaction to what happened)? Do you feel "butterflies" in your chest or stomach? Does that indicate to you a sense of nervousness or excitement?

Then check in with your emotions. Think about your options one by one. Do you feel excited, happy, or upset?

Check in mentally. Does your mind go to all of the problems that may arise as a result of a particular choice, or does it embrace all of the potential and possibilities that may present themselves?

Finally check in spiritually. "Ask" Source if this is the right direction or choice. Is it for your highest good? Go with the first impression that comes through. It may be a simple yes or no response. If nothing comes through, ask for a sign. The answer may come later in the day or later in the week, but as long as you pose the question, you will get an answer.

Exercise 3-17: To get clearer about the type of transformation you desire, try this exercise and write down the answers.

• What does the discomfort/frustration/confusion/anxiety look like? How is it manifesting currently on a daily basis?

• On a scale of 1 to 10, 1 being the least, what is the current level of discomfort?

• What is the underlying cause?

• What is the desired transformation? Be specific.

• How would it manifest on a daily basis?

• What is the physical level of the needed transformation?

• What is the emotional level of the needed transformation?

• What is the mental level of the needed transformation?

• What is the spiritual level of the needed transformation?

Once the nature of the transformation and its components are determined, it is then possible to ascertain the best way to address it.

Part III:
Staying Happy in the Present
While Creating Your Ideal Future

Introduction to Part III

I Want My Life to Be Different...

Do you wake up in the morning with the thought of *just getting through the day?* Do you exist task to task, hour to hour, waiting for the weekend or waiting for the next thing to happen that must be *dealt* with? The gift of life is not meant to be spent in despair and struggle. Challenges are there to teach and enlighten so you can get to the next level; living under a constant dark cloud is not truly living.

To get out from under that mindset, decide what you want your life to look like. When I hear someone say, "I want my life to be different," I ask her how she would want it to be different. Sadly, 95 percent do not know; they just know that the way their life is right now is not working for them.

Clarity is necessary to make significant changes in your life. You have the ability to create the life you want, but without really knowing what that looks like, it cannot be achieved.

Defining your life is the first step. Simply asking for "stuff" is not a definition. For example, you could say that you want to live in a big house and have four cars and loads of money, but does that really define your life? Are you envisioning your identity and purpose as a collector of expensive stuff? This type of focus is superficial and temporary, ripe for disappointment.

Exercise iii-1: Ask yourself these questions:

- What do you want your life to represent?

- What are you here to create?

- How do you want to be remembered?

- What makes you feel open and inspired?

- What impact do you want to have?
- How can you be in highest service to others?

To define your life and to envision it fully brings meaning and purpose. There is the potential for fulfillment when the definition includes the type of person you want to be, how you want to feel, and how you want to make others feel. Defining your life this way has the energy of depth and substance, of something that lasts beyond your physical presence. Do not allow the fear of change to stop you. Trust that the Universe will support your efforts when you are truly on the right path.

This approach enables you to identify what you are or want to become and, therefore, guides your behavior toward that end. The vision of your life serves to motivate you in certain directions, dissuade you from taking pathways that do not contribute to bringing about your vision, determine the way you treat others, and define how you view yourself. The clear vision is your roadmap to creating the life you want.

Our ability to create is what makes us powerful. Using that creativity is a large part of releasing what I call your Inner Magick, that unique gift you bring to the world. Ignoring your power and refusing to open your mind to grander possibilities and perspectives diminishes your energy. Expand the way you look at the world, yourself, and your life. You will find that you will feel more in control, things will start moving in positive directions, and you will be able to generate an alternate plan to use if you hit a roadblock.

How do you begin defining your life and gaining clarity? First, empty your mind of all preconceptions, all advice from others about what you should or should not do, and clear away your own expectations of what you thought your life should be. Next, open to Divine guidance and ask for clarity. Ask for a vision to come to you. It may come in a mental flash, or it may come through messages delivered in more subtle ways. Once you ask, be open to recognizing the guidance. It may be that several people in a row ask you to help them with a particular problem, or they may tell you that you are very gifted in a certain respect. Take note of these comments and understand the pattern.

Another way is to discuss it with a trusted friend or objective professional to gain important insights into what has been there all along; you were just unable to see past the clutter of thoughts, expectations, and disappointments. Everyone's path is unique. Begin seeking out your life vision now so you can achieve renewed purpose, deep meaning, and true contentment.

When you embrace your ability to create your life, you are no longer a victim of circumstance. You will begin to manifest what you envision, and your mind will be open to new ideas. Inspiration will come more frequently, and the world will be filled with possibilities rather than problems.

Stuck?

Are you stuck? Do you tell others that you do not like the way your life is, yet you do not have a vision of what you want or a plan to make the necessary changes to create something different? Have you become comfortable in your discomfort?

Here are some indicators that you are stuck:

1. You have been complaining about the same issues for at least a year, probably longer.

2. When seeking advice, your response to the helper tends to be "Yeah, but..." followed by all the reasons why the suggestion will not work.

3. Your favorite phrase is "I'll try" or "I'm trying." This is a passive response that does not move you further along the path.

4. If you frequently feel angry at your inability to change your life, the fear of change and reluctance to modify how you are perceiving the issue make you feel powerless.

5. When those around you tire of hearing the same problems over and over and suggest you do something to change it, your response is "I don't know how" or "I can't." Once again, this perspective denies the power you have within you.

If you have been in a mental and emotional rut for the last few years and have yet to find a way to get out, let me shed some light on how to move forward.

Feeling stuck is an opportunity to reassess what is important to you and to identify and prioritize what you want in your life. What you wanted a few years ago is probably not what serves you best in this stage of your life.

> **Exercise iii-2:** Clarify where you are right now and generate options that could move you beyond the "rut" you have been experiencing. Do not edit yourself, but simply write down all of the things that come to mind as potential alternatives to how you have been working and being until now.

Sometimes it is difficult to see clearly for yourself; after all, you are so close to the situation. If that is the case, work together with a trusted friend, relative, or professional to determine what is holding you back and how it is affecting your work, relationships, and time.

Many times, an alternate perspective is enough to create a shift in your consciousness to allow enough of an opening for you to get through to the other side. A fresh perspective can be gained through conversation with friends, reading inspirational material, or a quiet meditation session. If you choose a solitary path to break free of obstacles, ask for guidance from Divine Source to identify what is holding you back and the best way to overcome and move past it. Be open to all messages that come through.

The bottom line is that you create your life—for better or worse—and everything that is in your life right now is a result of your power to build it any way you want.

You ask, "Why would I create situations that make me miserable?" Good question. It does not have to be this way. If you build your life with every negative thought and fear, it produces difficulty and misery. Take this ability and construct something that you really want. It is a matter of shifting your perspective and your focus.

We are creators and each person has a unique way of conceptualizing and bringing into being what they focus on. Recently I went to a specialty shop to get a new battery for my watch. While the jeweler worked, I had the opportunity to look around the shop. It was dedicated to watches, many of which were high end. It was incredible to see how many different types, styles, and manufacturers of watches there were. The number of variations on the idea of a watch were extensive, and I could not help but think about the amazing way the human mind can run with so many different versions of the same item.

Exercise iii-3: Expanding your mind around a single concept opens the way for major transformation of an idea, situation, or yourself. Try it. Think about a single, simple object. It could be anything—a chair, a table, anything that comes to mind. Consider its form and function. How many ways are you able to see it in your mind's eye? Can you see it in different colors and shapes?

Now take a situation in your life; one that you have been looking at the same way for quite some time. How many ways can it be conceived? From how many different perspectives can it be seen? Take the opposite position from where you are currently. How does it feel to change the way you are seeing the situation? How might it affect the way you approach the situation in the future?

Finally, take an idea that's been bouncing around in your mind. Nail down the way you are perceiving it. Is it stopping you from taking the idea and running with it? Now shift the way you are looking at it. What modifications can you make that will open the way for progress?

Here are some strategies to help you shift from being stuck to embracing a more expansive viewpoint:

1. Each time a negative thought comes across your mind, counter it with a positive one. For example, "I'll never find another job" versus "The right opportunity is waiting for me."

2. Change the way you think of yourself. "No one wants me" versus "I have the power to attract the right relationship into my life."

3. Shift from thinking that you will do it "one day" to "I intend to start my journey toward X today."

4. Put a rubber band around your wrist, and every time you have a negative thought, catch yourself and snap the rubber band to

disrupt the flow of dark thoughts before they turn into what I call the anxiety death spiral.

5. When something undesirable occurs, ask "What is the lesson in this?" Seek to understand why the situation presented itself and what opportunity there is for growth.

6. Ask yourself what is holding you back; what are you really afraid of, and what is the worst thing that could happen if you break free from the constraints you have placed upon yourself?

7. Know that sometimes a delay proves beneficial, so do not confuse a well-timed delay with being stuck.

8. Take responsibility for where you are right now. It is not your parents' fault or anyone else's.

9. Take action. Those from whom you seek guidance cannot do it for you or offer a magic bullet to change your life. It is up to you to take charge of your life.

There are many ways to overcome being stuck. Awareness that you are stuck is a good first step to moving forward, and then you can begin the real work of breaking down the obstacles that hold you back. Remember, the only thing stopping you is yourself. It is time to get out of your own way. Make the decision to have the life you really want. It is never too late to make changes and to take control of your life. You have gifts to give to the world, and it is time to find out what those are so you can embrace your Inner Magick. Next time you feel stuck, exercise your mind by seeing how many alternatives and perspectives you can come up with; then watch how quickly you will be back on track and moving toward your goal.

Chapter 4: Your Personal Evolution: What Does It Mean to You?

If you are reading this book, you are seeking to improve yourself and your life. At this moment, you are spending time and effort on your personal development and, at the same time, you may be worrying about your performance, your ability to achieve your goals, and how others perceive you.

The Meaning of Personal Evolution

You may talk about evolving, but you may not have really defined what it means to do so. It is a change of perspective, a maturation, a shifting view of yourself, your role in the world, and in your life. It is finding ways to adapt to life and to improve the way relationships and situations are handled. To evolve means the deepening self-awareness and constant improvement of your skills and natural abilities. It is the ability to create your life in accordance with your unique vision. It is the discovery of the self, the meaning you put on your experiences, what you believe, and how it serves you.

How your beliefs, self-image, and self-knowledge affect you physically, emotionally, mentally, and spiritually is determined by testing new knowledge through experience and turning it into wisdom. Armed with this perspective, the judgment of others fades into the background, confusion dissipates, and your path becomes clear.

The Process of Personal Evolution

Self-awareness allows your reactions to evolve over time. Your beliefs and perspectives transform with each experience as you seek to validate what you already believe while possibly discovering that it is time to see things differently. You may start out seeking evidence that supports the existing framework / perspective, only to discover that the current construct of life no longer fits for your evolving sense of self.

If you do not feel ready for the next phase in the evolutionary process, rather than adapting and changing, you dig in and resist the shift. Fear of what will happen next, how relationships may change, how satisfaction with your current life may be altered, and not knowing what to do in response to the changes prevent forward movement. Recognize that it is a process of change and becoming. You go through cycles, like the moon does, starting in the dark, gradually brightening through enlightenment, reaching fulfillment in one aspect of your life and being excited about it, before the effect begins to wane and it is time to select a new goal or quest.

You have probably been through this process many times, although the pattern may not have been recognized. Your view of yourself and your place in the world have shifted over time as you seek to find your core self, that part of you that persists in all circumstances and relationships.

Shifting on the Path of Personal Evolution

Personal evolution is about achieving self-trust in the context of having the self-confidence to face change with excitement, wisdom, and the willingness to modify your underlying beliefs when appropriate.

In the quest for steady improvement, identifying the patterns of your personal cycles and process and then working with, instead of against, them makes life easier because you then function in accordance with your true nature. A sense of peace and flow replaces stagnation, agitation, and self-deprecation.

Rather than experiencing anxiety over not meeting the expectations of others, set your own expectations for yourself in living up to your potential in accordance with your natural gifts. Evolving in this way allows the cultivation of self-acceptance rather than beating yourself up for not being what others thought you should be. This false sense of the ideal self is the root of fear and anxiety. The limited perspective that held you back is banished, and an opening takes its place—a willingness to see yourself and the world in a different way.

Exercise 4-1: Every once in awhile, it is important to take a step back and reassess what you are striving for, what you want out of your life, and how things have changed over time. The process of evolving requires a periodic check-in with yourself. Ask, "Is the path I'm on still serving me and the things I want out of life?"

Your ability to change course in accordance with new experiences and new desires is the motivation that will keep you moving toward your goal. If it feels like you are bored or pounding your head against a wall, then it is probably time to reconsider your path and your ultimate goal.

In the work you do or the way you do the work you love, the opportunity to revisit the way you express your gifts can take new form and give a jolt of inspiration and creativity that may be lacking in the old way. Personal development forces new ways of looking at things, modifications of beliefs about the self and the world, and offers your self-expression a maturity and depth not possible in previous states of being.

Sometimes this shift from what you thought you wanted could feel like a failure. I have actually heard people say that. It is nothing of the sort! Let go of the guilt and embrace the ability to change your mind and open to change. To me, the mark of the successful person is the ability to reconsider his or her path and adjust accordingly.

This is not to say that jumping from one thing to the next with no sense of completion is the definition of success; that is the mark of a restless spirit who is unsure of what she wants. Rather it is a thoughtful contemplation of where you are in your life, your growth, and your circumstances, and how they can lead you closer to the ideal way of life and the means to create it.

You have a special gift. Seek to express it in its highest form by aligning with where you are in your development today.

Exercise 4-2: Journal about how your role and self-image have changed over time. Then create a vision, without limitations, of how you truly want to live your life. You will know that this new vision is in accordance with your true nature when it fosters a deep sense of peace, enabling you to breathe deeply and smile easily.

In the end (and there really is no end to personal evolution) your natural inclination toward continuous improvement makes you well-positioned to achieve your goals and a true sense of self. There will always be opportunities to learn and grow. Ultimately, those with this tendency look forward to the next bit of knowledge, the deeper journey into the self, and the sense of satisfaction that comes from knowing yourself and living in alignment with your true nature.

Finding Yourself in Order to Find Happiness

Are you still searching for who you are? For your purpose? For your true nature? Is it a matter of uncovering what is already there or creating the self in a way that meets an ideal of what you strive to become? I believe it is a combination.

Start by understanding your projected self, that is, the way others see you. Maintaining a false self is hard work and a recipe for unhappiness. An example of this is a woman I met who felt very anxious and depressed. She had backed herself into a corner.

"I can't keep it up anymore," she said, frowning and shaking her head.

"Keep what up?" I asked.

"Maintaining the image I have created. The way I want others to see me. They think I have major career success, lots of money, and that I have my act together. They think my life is perfect. The truth is, I have to work very hard to get what I have, I do not have as much money as they think I do, and it is not always easy. I need a break, but I don't want anyone to know that!"

This poor woman had worked herself into a frenzy worrying about what others thought of her and that she could not live up to the persona she had created for herself. I know her to be a wonderful, caring person who takes care of everyone around her. Among her many gifts are the ability to take charge of a situation and to make everything run smoothly—both at work and in taking care of her family's needs. She is the go-to person. She works hard and tries her best to do the right thing for everyone concerned. Aren't those the qualities that would attract genuine, healthy relationships?

Part of the problem is that she ultimately neglects herself and her needs in the process. Everyone, at one point or another, needs a break! This is ***not*** a sign of weakness. The other issue is that it is very stressful to try to live up to the expectations of others rather than basing your life on your own personal standards.

There are many things to consider in this situation. First, her self-image consisted only of external indicators of who she is. She had not felt her value and the gifts she brings to the world at a deep, inner level. Second, she no longer wanted to be thought of as her false image, but she saw no way to shift perceptions to her true self. Third, she could not engage her true self because she had been projecting this other image trying to be someone else for so long, that she had no idea who she truly was. As a result, she was not able to embrace her Inner Magick.

When people like you for superficial reasons—you are successful, you have money, you can do certain things for them—these are most likely not true friendships. These are not the people who will be honest with you and like you for yourself... or who will be there for you when *you* need help. They are around you because of what they can get from you. The question then becomes, why stress over what they think anyway? The importance that this woman had placed on others' opinions of her far exceeded their role in her life.

Money can be a defining aspect of self for some. Acknowledging that money is necessary to live and that most people need to work to survive, what is the amount of money you actually require to live a happy life? How much is sufficient?

If you find that you primarily strive to make money, but it is not a source of happiness for you, imagine that money is a non-issue. If you could do anything you wanted, knowing that you would be supported in the way you wanted... what would you strive for?

A friend of mine was on a cruise ship and met a woman who had a trust fund that provided her with a huge monthly income. He observed her looking bored, drinking lots of champagne, and not really enjoying herself.

Curious, he struck up a conversation and discovered that cruising and other leisure activities were her entire life. There was no goal, no work, no learning, and no striving! He told me that she seemed like the unhappiest person he had ever met. In the same vein, I watched a documentary about trust fund babies who were at a loss for what to do with their lives. Given that money was no object, they were clueless as to what to do with the time, or the money, at their disposal. When one of them asked their father what he should do with his life, the father suggested that he "collect something."

So if, beginning tomorrow, you never had to work again, what would you do? What would your goals be? What cause would you champion? Goals and the process of attaining them keep you vibrant and purposeful. Strive for something beyond money to give your life meaning. The value of a life cannot be measured in dollars.

In order to make the shift and be comfortable coming into your true self, the first step is to decide that you are ready to shed false images and beliefs about yourself. Then, let go of the idea that your value is directly proportionate to what others think of you or how much money you have. Finally, get to know yourself and what makes you happy. Incorporate what you discover into your life in a way that allows you to envision an ideal life aligned with who you truly are.

When you live a life in accordance with your true self, it is amazing how much calmer and centered you will feel. You are able to handle all of your obligations and responsibilities even better, and you will be stronger so you can take care of those who are really important to you. Those who do not resonate with your true self will gently fall away, and you will realize that their absence does not really affect you.

Exercise 4-3: List the consistencies in your nature, the things you have naturally done or enjoyed since childhood, the things people often tell you are your best and worst attributes. Then write down the characteristics you wish to attain. Look around you at people you admire. What are some of the traits that make you feel drawn to them? Which of those would you like to embody within yourself?

Now take a look at the similarities and disparities of the two lists. Do they line-up pretty well, or are there gaps between who you feel you are and who you would like to become?

You come into this life with certain tendencies, qualities, and energies. Life is a journey of the self, a path designed to learn certain lessons through experience and the understanding gained through it. It is possible to modify behavior, thought patterns, and emotional responses. There is free will and, therefore, choice in the ways you express yourself. At the same time, certain traits and abilities are hardwired, making each person unique and some choices out of alignment with our nature.

For example, some have astounding gifts for artistic expression, but not all. Even with years of lessons, they may never produce the images they see in their mind's eye. Yet others have a natural gift in this regard and, with or without formal lessons, are capable of great achievement in the arts. Sticking with this example, if you love the act of creating art, but you have limited artistic capacity, you can still do it, albeit not professionally.

Understanding your true nature includes embracing limitations and focusing your energy on developing your natural gifts. In the process, you gain self-knowledge and, ultimately, happiness, from being able to revel in who you are.

Can Your Future Be Predicted?

The world is in a constant state of flux. Each time a change occurs, everything it touches, directly and indirectly, also changes. There are too many variables to take into account and too many shifts that can take place to make an accurate prediction that stands the test of time. Not everything is in your control. By understanding these shifting energies, you can stay flexible in your thinking and make decisions that will enable you to move your life forward.

Many people consult psychics to find out what their future holds. They want reassurance, they want the intuitive consultant to tell them what will happen so they feel more in control, and they want good news. We are creators of our future; any predictions made during a reading can be changed by making a decision or by someone else taking an action after the reading takes place.

The best use of a reading is to provide an objective perspective, minus the drama. Rather than looking for predictions, use a reading as a way of tapping into the current energies going on in your life and the obstacles you are facing that need to be addressed. Make the most of your reading and ask questions like, "What is blocking me from getting what I want out of life?" or "What is the most important thing for me to know right now?" Stay open to the answers and consider how they may apply. When you have an intuitive consultation, use your time and the information you receive wisely. Retain your power and create your ideal life.

To predict something is to tell it in advance, to see it before it happens, or to gather indicators and determine what is to come. The act of prediction is attempted on many levels. For those seeking life guidance, tools of divination are used, such as tarot and astrology, or aid is sought by psychic means. On a mundane level, tools such as weather tracking and geological instruments are used to predict storms, earthquakes, and volcanic eruptions. One is on the intuitive level, and one is scientific. In both cases, information is gathered by whatever means the predictor is using, and then the probable outcome is determined based on that information.

Recently, weather scientists predicted a major snowstorm to hit our area based on current weather patterns. There were storm warnings, people rushed the supermarkets to stock up, and salt trucks stood at the ready. Everyone was worried about losing power. Mother Nature changed her mind, and the weather patterns shifted, moving out into the ocean. We got about an inch of snow. All of that panic for nothing.

This can happen with a reading, as well. The practitioner predicts dire circumstances, or even happy ones that elate the client, and then it may or may not happen. The client can make choices that change the course of his or her life. This is called Free Will, and it is the primary ingredient in determining what will come next. You change your mind, gain new knowledge, or make a decision that changes the course of everything. Based on choices, the flow of energy stays on course or shifts to a different outcome.

We cannot even predict how we, ourselves, will feel about something a few months or years from now. I remember my whole perspective changing between ages twenty-seven and twenty-eight, then again at thirty-five, and then again at forty, etc., and everything I thought I wanted changed dramatically. My decisions were then based on that new mindset, which changed the course of my life. Admittedly, people have come to me years after a reading to let me know that everything I told them was true and accurate. That's because I showed them the energies that were around them at the time, as well as the trajectory their life was moving in. If they liked it, they chose to stay on the current path; if not, they shifted it. I saw what they could not see, and then they made appropriate decisions for themselves.

There are way too many variables to predict a final outcome accurately, just like Mother Nature in the snow example. Once in awhile, an astounding prediction comes true; I attribute this to the variables coming together in such a way that they become locked in. The Universe decided that this event must take place in order for other events to follow.

It is difficult to see ourselves and our lives because we are too close to them. We cannot be objective. This is where a reading is best used—so we can understand the current energies and how they impact people and circumstances. At the same time, the Universe can decide to intervene at any point and take things in a completely different direction. This is when going with the flow is important, for it will likely show you something that could not have been anticipated. If you could see the future consistently and accurately, it would take away your motivation to strive toward a desired outcome. It would also limit what the Universe could offer in the way of new opportunities that arise based on shifts occurring in places and with people you have no awareness of. In many ways, we create our future, with some spice thrown in by the Universe.

Given this, focus on being your own guide and creator based on self-awareness, self-trust, and self-actualization. Expand your definition of creativity and open to your personal creative abilities. When you manifest something in your life, you have created it; your intention brought it into being. With each choice you make and every thought you have, your life is shaped and directed. Be consciously aware of how your creative energies are directed to bring forth what you truly want in your life.

Rejoice in the good fortune of others. There is plenty for everyone, so there is no need for envy or resentment. Each of us can have exactly what we want without creating lack for others, so do not hesitate to open to receive and to create.

Every choice you make creates your future. Whether the choice is to take action or to do nothing, it is a decision that you make. I have seen many people make choices and blame others for the results, yet take credit that it was all their doing when they succeed. Taking responsibility includes doing so for all that is in your life rather than picking only some aspects.

There are many who feel that life is predestined, that we have no real choice as far as the hand we are dealt in this life. Yet even in a card game, we can choose which cards to toss back or we can ask for more cards. In astrology or in tarot, certain energies are present that can be used to our advantage if the choice is made to do so, or even to resist the energies inherent in the current circumstances to create difficulty and anxiety. By making a choice, the future shifts and the probabilities for certain outcomes are modified.

It is up to each of us to follow our inner guidance, and even to accept Divine Will or not, when choosing the life we want to live. If you have ever thought back to a decision that changed the course of your life and wished—or not—that you had chosen differently, you understand that free will played a part in the life you live today.

Is it better to live in the moment or plan ahead? Some say one strategy is better than the other. I believe that balance is the key to all endeavors. Staying in the moment allows you to limit distractions and focus in order to complete the task at hand. Being in the present is a meditative practice that reduces anxiety by attending only to what is happening in that moment.

Planning ahead and strategizing for the long term allows you to set goals and to envision your growth opportunities and what you want your life to look like. Once you have the vision of the future firmly in your mind, return to the present to accomplish the tasks required to get you further down the path toward your ultimate desire.

When feeling overwhelmed with what is already happening in your life, it can be difficult to envision long-term goals. That is when staying in the present can help you clear up the current issues so that your mind has the bandwidth to think beyond current obstacles. When you conceptualize what you ultimately want in your life, it is easier to move past the blocks of the present.

You have the ability to go with the flow, to ride the energetic wave, to understand how you affect your future, and to create a vision of what you want your life to look like. It is time to take a step back and understand how what you do, think, and feel affects you and those around you. Creating a vision also requires a sense of self-control, self-discipline, mindfulness, and conscious choice over habit and complacency. In addition, a heightened awareness of the energies that surround you, that are within you, and ways to flow with them is a necessary condition for personal success.

With this awareness comes the understanding that it takes years, if not a lifetime, to understand fully oneself and one's place in the Universe. Healing yourself comes before healing others, and letting go of all that holds you back—beliefs, history, negative emotions, and thoughts—comes in order to create true happiness.

The time of magic bullets, quick fixes, giving away power, and wishcraft are behind us. Seeing that we create our future rather than attempting to predict it, and using systems of metaphysics such as tarot and astrology for self-exploration, for identifying blocks to progress, and for connection to the divine, is part of the shift toward the happiness perspective. Taking control of your future requires a sense of responsibility for what is being created. Developing the natural intuitive gifts you possess to receive guidance and learning to use them to navigate daily life are parts of the happiness mindset.

Spirituality goes beyond any religion or prescribed way of being regardless of tradition. It is a personal relationship and connection to the Divine that requires the seeker to define its nature and his or her relationship to it on a very deep and personal level.

The Law of Infinite Universes states that each person sees his universe or world a different way; therefore, no two people have identical worldviews. It is time to determine what your personal Universe includes and how you want to experience it. To sum it up, define the divine, receive divine downloads, understand your relationship with yourself, discover the uniqueness of the Self, and act in accordance with your true nature. Learn to interact effectively in the physical plane in which you live and go into a deeper connection with the Divine and with the Self. With the ability to create our future, there is no need for prediction.

The Keys to Staying Happy in the Present While Creating Your Ideal Future

Do you find yourself saying, "I'll be happy when (fill in the blank)"—when I get a better job, make more money, get married, have a great significant other, have time for myself... and the list goes on?

In the search for the path to success, destiny, happiness, love, or whatever takes you closer to your goals, few seem to find their way. You may rely on someone else to take you where you think you want to go as when a significant other is handed the responsibility for your happiness. Or maybe you feel that by gaining a certain job, dollars in the bank, or a romantic conquest, that all will be well, and then you can relax.

Take a look at your life. Be objective when doing so. How much would you really change? You may already be living 90 percent of your dream and simply not appreciating it. On the other hand, you may have many unfulfilled dreams and desires, but you are not taking steps to move closer to your goals. Or you may just choose to maintain your life the way it is, yet complain about the things you lack.

Finding your way takes work and requires that you take responsibility for your happiness and/or success. Only you can make your life the way you want it by way of your choices, actions, and self-knowledge. What it is that you really want? Start there, and you will be much closer to finding where to take the first step toward finding your ideal life.

Anticipating the future but never seeming to attain the vision causes anxiety. You have tried doing vision boards, imagining your ideal life, and saying daily affirmations, yet what you are asking for does not materialize. It can result in giving up because the "when" never seems to happen. Generally, the Universe does not bestow additional blessings until the current ones are gratefully acknowledged.

So while you are in the process of envisioning your ideal life and taking steps toward it, here are some ways you can be happy in your present life, even though it may not be the ideal situation.

1. **Be grateful for everything that is in your life right now.** Gratitude produces joy; appreciation for the little things adds up to a whole lot of wonderful. Make a list of what you are grateful for—health, roof over your head, inner strength during a difficult time, etc. Also, recognize that each and every experience holds a lesson that gets you closer to your goals. Whatever is happening right now is pertinent to your growth and necessary to get to the next level of your development. Get as much out of these experiences as possible, and use them to your advantage going forward, all the while being grateful for the lesson.

2. **Know what you want.** Just saying that you want things to be different while not being sure what that looks like keeps you stuck in dismay. Having a clear vision of what you are aiming for enables you to set small, attainable goals that move you closer to your ideal life.

3. **Have a purpose.** The quest for purpose can be daunting if it is conceptualized as something so big that it is scary and difficult to put your finger on. Cut it down to understanding what your purpose is within the moment. With each interaction, ask yourself what your intention is and in what way you are serving the other person, as well as yourself. Soon you will see a pattern that serves as the larger picture of your purpose. In the meantime, this exercise gives significance to your daily experiences, and meaning is a key to finding happiness.

4. **Ask "Why?"** Piggy-backing on the idea of purpose, ask yourself "why" you are doing something or "why" you want it. The "why" is your personal story, your brand of living, and the reason behind everything you do, say, or believe. Understanding "why" allows you to reflect and

determine whether the underlying reasons are motivating and inspiring or detrimental and debilitating. If you find a lower energy reason in the "why," such as jealousy, revenge, depression, anxiety, etc., then shift it to a higher vibration by modifying the "why" to an uplifting reason such as: it is something you enjoy doing, it benefits others in some way, or it gets you closer to your goals.

5. **Know yourself and your special gifts.** They are the value you bring to the world. Your gifts are most apparent when you are expressing yourself effortlessly. This is tricky since when it is effortless on your part, the value seems less. Your unique abilities may be very difficult for others to emulate, hence the reason they are your particular gifts and why they have value. Discover how best to use them in the present, and bring them into your ideal future.

6. **Start doing what you love now.** Say you struggle to get up in the morning because you do not want to go to your boring or stressful job. Paying the bills is important, so having to stick with a job you dislike is easier if you have something on the side that you enjoy or that is part of what you are building for the future. Yes, after a long day at work, you are probably drained of any energy to put toward the thing you enjoy doing. You will be surprised how much energy is generated when you have something to look forward to after work or on your days off. A fun hobby, volunteer work, attending a class or seminar, writing a blog—something creative or worthwhile goes a long way toward a happy present while you are building your future.

7. **Evaluate your relationships.** Those who take you for granted, drain you, constantly complain, are naysayers when you talk about your aspirations, and are only focused on themselves, diminish your capacity for happiness. Minimize or eliminate your time with the *poor-me* people. Hang out with people who are motivated, happy with their lives, interested in the potentials and possibilities in life, and are continuous learners. This type of interaction is energizing and inspirational, sparking new ideas and confidence in your ability to accomplish your goals.

8. **Stay in the moment.** Do not pine for the future and the time when you will finally be happy. Enjoy the moment, no matter how insignificant it seems. Take in the smells of nature, put down the cell phone and talk to the person you are with, pay attention to preparing and eating your food or to the experience in the restaurant. Practice enjoying the little things in life and you will be positioned to enjoy your future success even more.

9. **Strive for peace, not for stuff.** Money is not the key to happiness, although it is necessary for food, shelter, and clothing. Decide what kind of lifestyle you want that will bring you peace rather than a Rolex. Simplify your idea of what you need in your life. The more stuff you have, the more

maintenance it requires, and the more stress that is in your life. The recipe for happiness includes knowing what makes you feel calm and comfortable. The simple things—a comfy sweater, watching a movie with friends, or a walk in the park—can be the foundation of a happy life, both now and going forward.

10. **Tap into a cheerful vibration.** Bring joy and light into your personal or work space to enhance your energy and raise your vibration. You can do this by opening the curtains and letting sunshine indoors, by performing a spiritual cleansing with prayer, blue sage and sweet grass, and by using plants and flowers to maintain the uplifted energy. The energy of yellow and orange flowers can be enhanced by placing them in front of mirrors. Make sure to remove them when they begin to wilt to avoid the energy of decay. The cheerful vibration of sunshine can be achieved even on a rainy day by thinking happy thoughts, focusing emotional energies on emanating love from your center, and by laughter. Listen to upbeat music with inspiring lyrics to shift your vibrational frequency up. Bring this joy to others by entering their space with a smile and filled with happiness for the connection. When visiting someone, bring a gift that represents fun and good cheer, and present it to the host. Boost your high spirits and create joyful vibrational reserves by playing outdoors in the sunshine, being grateful, and making the most of your life.

You may be closer to creating your ideal future than you think, and if not, incorporating the ten strategies above into your present life can go a long way in cultivating happiness while you strive toward making your dreams come true.

Is Your Current Lifestyle Sustainable?

That is, can you continue living with your current mindset, belief system, or level of stress and anxiety, and stay healthy while achieving your goals? Are you making your life harder than it has to be? Do you tend to make a big deal out of everything?

Modern life can be complicated. We are always plugged in, always on the go, able to work from anywhere, and actively maintaining lots of relationships both in person and online. Think of all of the things you do out of obligation. Think of the times when you went someplace to relax, yet could not bring yourself to turn off your cell phone. Gandhi said, "The simplification of life is one of the steps to inner peace. A persistent simplification will create an inner and outer wellbeing that places harmony in one's life."

Exercise 4-4: Make a list of activities you do in a typical day. What can be removed or done less often to simplify your day? Getting rid of certain habits like smoking can simplify your life since, in most cases, you have to go out of your way to find a place to smoke when not at home. Turn off your cell phone when driving or walking in the park. Focus on the environment or the activity you are doing and limit distractions. Release relationships that no longer serve you. Remove any activities that create chaos or disruption.

Think about your daily life, the choices you make, and the activities you engage in. Are you getting enough sleep? Are you drinking too much alcohol or smoking too much? Do you frequently ask "what if" questions that put you in a state of anxiety? Do you feel overwhelmed most of the time? Pay attention to how your body feels when you participate in certain activities and relationships. What kind of energy do you sense relating to it? Does it feel harmonious? Do you feel uplifted or exhausted? Recognize that you choose what is in your life and how you feel toward it. If you feel time-limited and stressed, your choices are creating that energy in your life. Strive to engage people and participate in activities that create a sense of peace and fulfillment.

Now think about alternate choices you can make that will reduce heightened, overindulgent states. Let us take feeling overwhelmed, for example. Look at how much you take on. Is it necessary? You might say yes if it has to do with work. At the same time, is your sense of being overwhelmed being exacerbated by what you choose to do after work?

Exercise 4-5: List everything you do from the moment you leave work. If you do not have a regular job, list all of the activities that make up a normal day. What can you do less often? Are you creating more stress than you have to? Restrict or eliminate activities that have no reward of any kind to you personally and assess your return on time investment. If they are necessary activities, then find resources to help you manage them rather than taking everything on by yourself.

One of the stressors may be relationships. Managing many relationships means managing loads of interactions. How many of these relationships are healthy? How many of these relationships do you really enjoy?

Exercise 4-6: Make a list of the people who are in your life. Make a column for a one-word description of the relationship. It might say spouse, children, or friend; then rate these with descriptors such as enjoy, obligation, work, or stressful. Target those with descriptors like "obligation" or "stressful." Decide to reduce your relationship load by spending less time with or eliminating these relationships completely. In this way, you will reduce your stress level and have some time for yourself.

Staying in a constant state of aggravation, stress, anxiety, or feeling overwhelmed is not sustainable. It will result in physical illness, exhaustion, depression, resentment, and/or anger. Sense when you need to disengage and unplug; then take time to do something you enjoy, by yourself. Read a book, walk in the woods, write in your journal; whatever it is that takes you out of the normal routine and gives you a breather.

Balance is the key to sustainability. You will feel happier, healthier, and more energized on a regular basis.

Live a Balanced Life

You are probably thinking, "Are you kidding me? Is it even possible to live a balanced life? And if so, what needs to be sacrificed to achieve it?" The answers are, yes, it is possible and the only thing you will need to give up is anxiety and angst.

With life being so demanding, most folks find themselves choosing between getting things done, helping and serving others, and working more and playing less. The idea of fitting in time for what you personally enjoy is almost laughable. It is hard to imagine how this could work without having obligations fall by the wayside.

Nature demonstrates a delicate balance in the ecosystem with one life form dependent on the health of the other and all dependent upon the health of the planet. In the same way, it is important to maintain an internal balance. A state of internal imbalance creates illness, injury, restlessness, and emotional and mental dysfunction. The key to attaining balance is creating harmony among the different aspects of your life, as well as within yourself.

Living a happy life requires balance above all. When behaviors, thoughts, and emotions go to extremes, or when you focus on one aspect of life only, it takes you off center. When this imbalance occurs, objectivity is lost.

Power starts at the core, at the center of your being. Think of a pendulum. It always starts in the center of the circle in which it can swing based on the length of the chain or string it hangs from. The pendulum is able to swing in any direction within that circumference and then returns to center. It never stays stuck in one direction; it always ends up back in the center. When you go in one direction or another, when you feel an extreme emotion, or when you focus your attention for too long on one thing, it takes you off balance. This can happen with thoughts you have about yourself, the world, or relationships. Strive to balance these extremes so you can stay centered.

If you find yourself participating in negative self-talk the majority of the time, take time to consider all of the things you have done well. Life changes; balance is necessary to ride the wave of fear, uncertainty, and difficulty that arises from time to time. Be versatile and adaptable when challenges arise. Periodically shift your focus to regain balance. Know that you are able to transcend the moment and derive valuable lessons to be used in the future.

The physical, emotional, mental, and spiritual aspects of yourself and your life work together, each affecting the other. Where there is an imbalance, there is disharmony, which results in negative emotions and general disturbances in your life. If your physical body is out of balance, it results in illness and the lack of energy to perform all of the daily tasks on your schedule. The physical body is your foundation, and so disruption at this level creates negative emotions such as anger, anxiety, and depression. An imbalance in the mental state can also negatively impact emotional stability. If the spiritual component is missing, then it is more difficult to balance the other three.

Balance these aspects of yourself as follows:

- **Physical:** Healthy diet and exercise. Promptly address medical issues. Get check-ups.

- **Emotional:** Dump negativity into the ground [see Appendix] on a regular basis. Do not allow it to accumulate. Avoid complaining and count your blessings.

- **Mental:** Catch negative self-talk and replace it with optimistic statements and self-encouragement. Soothe your thoughts with peaceful imagery, such as a calm lake.

- **Spiritual:** Take time to walk in nature, contemplate life in general, and connect to the Divine essence.

With all four of these aspects in balance, it is easier to balance your schedule and activities. You will have more energy and less stress. Review your weekly tasks and demands, whether they are work or personal, and eliminate or find another way to address those that create stress and disharmony. Schedule time for yourself and luxuriate in a tub, get a massage, or meditate. It is okay to be kind to yourself. And you will achieve balance before you know it.

Chapter 5: The Lessons That Lead to Happiness

Being taken out of your comfort zone is a great way to quickly learn lessons on living in happiness that may have taken a lot longer to get. When change happens, there is a choice to resist and make things harder than they have to be, or to enjoy the moment and see what new adventures await.

Here are the primary lessons I received on an unexpected and extended trip to Kauai.

Lesson 1: Go With the Flow!

After a month of anticipation and a week's notice, my husband got word that he was to manage a project in Hawaii. The project was open-ended, and he would be away for at least a month, so I decided to go with him. Being a planner, I started making my list of things we needed to do to prepare for our trip, including getting taxes done in early February. Rather than succumbing to the pressure of the tight timeframe, I focused on each item, confident that it would all work out by the deadline. Amazingly, it all got done, including the purchase of two one-way plane tickets.

In the past, any trip I have ever taken had a definite beginning and a definite ending, marked by the flight dates of round trip plane tickets. For the first time, I had no idea what my schedule would be for at least a month, maybe more. The project was extended three times before I finally made my return flight arrangements almost two months later. Happiness was maintained through the practice of allowing and going with the flow rather than resisting and stressing over changes.

> **Exercise 5-1:** How are you blocking your flow by trying to control every aspect of the process/path of your life? What can you allow today that you may have tried to control yesterday?

Lesson 2: Listen to Those With Experience!

The Universe plucked me out of my world and plopped me down in a whole new environment and circumstance. Starting at the airport, continuous loop videos warned tourists of riptides, crumbling mountainsides near hiking trails, and other hazards on the island; they made it clear that Kauai has awesome beauty and deadly natural events, so it seemed clear that it is best to heed the warnings of those who live there.

No matter how many warnings were put on TV, on videos at the airport, and at car rental places, reports of people drowning or having hiking mishaps were regular news stories. Most were tourists who did not listen and thought they knew better. Teenagers do this often, thinking that their parents do not know anything, only to find out much later in life that, in fact, they do. Ignoring sound advice is not the same as maintaining sovereignty; it can be a dangerous choice. Use common sense when you choose to go against information that may save you time and, possibly, your life.

Exercise 5-2: What advice are you ignoring from those who have walked the path you seek to tread?

Lesson 3: Adapt, Acclimate, and Learn to Live Without Your Stuff!

With an Internet connection and my computer, I could still work and keep in touch with family, friends, and clients. Given this grand opportunity for a real change, I decided to let go of the things that dictate my normal routine and to open to whatever I was supposed to learn while in Kauai. Surprisingly, it was relaxing to live with a pared down version of my clothes and possessions. I could have actually done with even less than I brought and discovered the efficiency of doing laundry in multiple machines at the laundromat.

The time difference was also an adjustment, being behind Eastern Standard Time by five hours, and then discovering that there is no Daylight Savings Time in Hawaii, so then being behind EDT by six hours. Opening my emails at 7 a.m. in Hawaii gave me a full day's worth by then. I acclimated to the time difference faster than expected regarding both work and sleep cycle.

When asking the Universe for a message for the time I spent in Kauai, all I heard was "Relax and heal." It was then I realized that it was a time to take a step back, clear, unwind, and consider the path I needed to follow in a more focused way. It is important to do this periodically, yet it is easier to continue on the hamster wheel, checking things off the list, and creating more and more to-dos. My nature is to plan, so I will schedule downtime at regular intervals in the future.

Exercise 5-3: Ask yourself what you think you need, but could probably do without. Seek to simplify your life. Periodically reevaluate your path and revise accordingly.

Lesson 4: Understand a Different Culture and Way of Being!

The vibe in Kauai is laid back and friendly, which is a much different approach than on the East Coast where we want everything now and there is an expectation of immediate results. No one is in a hurry, which is good, since there is only one main road with only one lane going in each direction.

There is a sense that things can change at any time by virtue of storms and other natural events, so there's no need to sweat the small stuff, and going with the flow is a way to stay grounded and centered. Many folks we spoke with were there when Hurricane Iniki ripped through the island, and they lost power for three months. Remember the storm scene in the movie *Jurassic Park*? That was actual footage of Hurricane Iniki taken by the camera crew of that film. It was Iniki that is said to have released the chickens that proliferate all over the island.

The idea of concentrating on one thing at a time rather than having multiple balls in the air became appealing and helped me trim my project load and my approach to work. It is a practice I have continued. The repetitious barrage of waves against the shore seems to symbolize life on the island. Some stay to feel that unrelenting sense of calm and peace, while others come for a short respite and then, refreshed, go back to their lives with renewed vigor.

Staying open to seeing other cultures and ways of being and honoring their perspective gives pause to how life is approached day-to-day. It allows an opening to consider a different way of being beyond the one you have grown used to and an adjustment to how life is viewed and responded to. Prejudice comes from a lack of understanding and appreciation for the marvelous variety of cultures and ways of being available for us to experience.

Exercise 5-4: What judgment have you imparted lately that prevented you from fully experiencing a particular culture or belief system?

Lesson 5: Be Respectful!

The Hawaiians have a deep respect for nature (the awesome beauty and deadly riptides) and for the sacred sites scattered around the island. Everyone can benefit from this important idea, which was emphasized when seeing the ancient Hawaiian temples called *heiau* with signs all around that said *kapu*, meaning forbidden/taboo. This was to honor the area and to preserve the *mana* or power of the area. Think of all of the "sacred" or "power" sites in your area and how many people have tread through them without regard for what they stand for or for the people who established them, thereby diminishing the energy and disrespecting the space.

Approaching all nature as sacred ground is a show of respect, of reverence, and of humility, understanding that the land was here before us, and its energies are best left intact. We can benefit from these natural power centers if we use them in this way. Someone recently said to me that it was difficult to feel the energy of the vortexes of Sedona with fifty people standing around trying to do the same thing. One of my students mentioned that the area at Ringing Rocks in Pennsylvania felt sad because everyone was just banging away at the stones trying to hear them ring without any respect for the stones' history.

Being in nature and showing respect for it increases happiness since natural environments and sacred places willingly give vitality to those who approach them with care. In this way, the role of guardian is established; when preserving nature through respect and esteem, an opening occurs, connecting you to the environment and the power held within.

Exercise 5-5: How can you increase respect for natural environments, the sacred space of others, and even your own sacred spaces?

Lesson 6: Let Go—Make Room for the New

Working in my garden is relaxing, as well as a place to tap into a wealth of simple truths that can be applied to life beyond the rose bushes. As I pull weeds, I notice that some are closer to the surface and easily plucked from the ground, others send out strong roots that have to be pried up, and still others could be pulled with minor effort, yet send out rhizomes into the rest of the plants.

Beneath them, there are plants I want to preserve and allow to thrive. This activity makes me think about aspects of ourselves, those we wish to remove and others we desire to maintain. Weeding the garden of the self is challenging when there are deep-rooted issues that take time to understand and clear, while others are easily shed. At times, a negative thought or belief may send out shoots that affect other thoughts and serve to diminish motivation or self-esteem.

So how can you preserve the best of yourself and identify the issues that need to be plucked to allow the positive aspects to flourish? Let go of the old to make room for the new!

Letting go is hard. We hold on to things from the distant past and continue to add to them as we walk the path of life. We choose to keep experiences, along with the feelings they incite, for better or worse. Usually, it works against us, as the most likely energies we hold are those that are detrimental. These have the biggest impact on us. Times when we made a mistake at work or in school, chose the wrong relationship, did not take advantage of an opportunity, disappointed someone, or even times when others did or said something hurtful toward us, tend to stick in our minds.

Recalling upsetting moments can cause those moments to have the same effect they did when they actually happened. They are recorded physically, emotionally, and mentally. The process of remembering a difficult time makes our bodies tense, our heart race, our emotions flare with anger or dampen with sadness, and our thoughts go through the same paces and lines of negative thinking. This is why holding on to negative experiences and the energies they contain is detrimental to our wellbeing. It is like watching an upsetting movie over and over.

Yet we cling to these experiences as if releasing them would cause us to lose a piece of ourselves. As if in persisting in remembering, we are actively doing something about it. As if holding on to them ensures that we will never make the same mistakes again. The fault in this logic is that the damaging effects far outweigh the good. The self-deprecating beliefs that started when the incident happened continue to be reinforced each time the event is called forth.

The other difficulty produced by hanging on to the old is that fresh energies that are aligned with our current desires and ideal lifestyle are unable to come in. Space needs to open in order for the new energies to have a place; a void must be created. The thought of having a void within the self is scary on its own. That sense of the unknown makes us shudder and takes us off center. What will it be replaced with? Will it be worse than what is there now? After all, we grow used to discomfort and allow it to continue due to its familiarity.

While we can agree that it is best to let go of the old way of thinking brought on by past circumstances, it is much more difficult to clear it from our consciousness than simply deciding not to think about it anymore. It has become embedded into our psyche, our cells, and our emotional memory. Our senses pull in sights, sounds, smells, textures, and tastes that may trigger an uncomfortable memory. A feeling of heaviness may accompany the review of the negative situation.

One of the most detrimental acts one can commit toward oneself is to hold on to the negativity in the form of negative emotions, experiences, and thoughts. Holding on to the inconsiderate or hurtful behaviors of others causes upset and despair in our lives.

We hold memories based on experiences, desires, fears, and dreams. Some memories are accurate and others are an automated mind message that fills in gaps between what we wanted the situation to be and the reality of what it truly was. As we grow and learn, we have the opportunity to re-examine what has transpired in our lives and how it served to shape us and our relationships with friends and family members. As the veil of disillusion is lifted, we are able to see clearly the actuality of our relationships and how they affect our lives. When the truth is revealed, it may be harsher than you would like, or it may be more pleasant. Either way, it allows us to transform what we thought we knew and to create a new self-image or mindset. We are not obligated to maintain delusional memories of relationships or any other experiences.

Exercise 5-6: You have permission to release the old, the outmoded, and the inaccurate, and to embrace that which allows you to expand beyond your old way of being. Do not allow yourself to be held firmly to a belief or a relationship when you know intuitively it is not healthy for you to do so. Seek that which transforms outmoded patterns into fresh perspectives.

Let us look at some examples of situations that are held onto:

- An adult holds on to something his parents did when he was a child that he blames as the reason for his unhappiness or lack of success today.

- Adult children decide to withhold grandchildren or make decisions they feel best for their life that do not include their parents.

- Indiscretions or infidelities committed by one's romantic partner.

In every case, the focus is on the behavior of someone else and that is being made into the focus of one's life.

Regardless of how painful, hurtful, or frustrating, it is time to let it go. Some say to forgive, and that is up to you, but I prescribe choosing to let go instead. In the case of parents, consider that our parents are in our lives to help us learn certain lessons. It is up to us to get the lesson, regardless of how their behavior delivers the message.

So what is the secret of letting go of the past in order to make room for the new? Keep the lesson and lose the negativity associated with it! We do not need the entire circumstance in our memory banks to have total recall of the valuable lesson held within.

Get started on clearing some of the outmoded ways of thinking and begin the healing and revitalization of our life:

1. **Stop talking about the disturbing situation.** Frequently talking about a negative occurrence allows it to dig an even deeper hole into your consciousness. Say we are in a toxic relationship or hold on to the memory of one. We talk about it to anyone who will listen. The situation's energy is enhanced when it is continuously brought up. Enlisting the help of friends to alert us when we bring it up can help us break the habit. Let go of reinforcing the situation with conversation. Bring forth fresh energy by getting out of the current toxic relationship or by remembering the lesson of knowing when it is time to leave from the last situation.

2. **Stop the thought in its tracks.** Wear a rubber band on the wrist, and when the thought comes up, snap the rubber band and

mentally yell, "Stop!" Let go of the tendency to beat yourself up again and again each time the memory is recalled. Bring forth new, positive thoughts about the times, both in the past and in the present, when you did something right at work or helped someone when they needed it most.

3. **Dump the old energy into the ground.** The accumulation of negativity is overwhelming and must be dumped on a regular basis. Stand on a piece of ground outside or over your shower drain. Release every negative thought, emotion, and memory held within. Allow all the stress of the day, all worry, doubt, and fear to drain from the body, starting at the head and moving all the way down the arms, torso, legs, out the bottoms of the feet, and into the ground. Let the negative energy flow into the ground (Mother Earth will cleanse it) until there is nothing left. Let go of everything that no longer serves you until you feel empty. Bring forth fresh Earth energy by moving ten feet away and pulling bright orange light from the center of the planet to fill in the newly opened space.

Letting go does not mean negating our past or the people in it. Rather, it is a clearing and a rejuvenation that can only occur when there is a willingness to release resentment, hurt, anger, distress, pain, and humiliation. Once this happens, the lesson is retained without the harmful side effects to make room for the glorious energies that await.

Lesson 7: Be Grateful—Harness the Power of Gratitude

Gratitude is an essential component in daily life, to give thanks for all that is in your life. Whether you perceive what you have as welcomed or unwelcomed, everything you have is in your life for a reason.

This mindset gives the opportunity to consider the lessons inherent in the circumstances you face. Successfully navigating the issue and understanding the deeper meaning of why it is in your life enables you to move past it in a way that permanently removes the old, destructive patterns.

When finding it difficult to be grateful—when things seem to be piling on top of you—volunteer for a cause that serves those whose lives are even more challenging than your own or watch TV programs that focus on people overcoming overwhelming physical challenges and situations. In context, your perspective will shift, and you will likely give thanks for your own circumstances.

Celebrate each and every positive occurrence, no matter how small, and your mind will develop a habit of seeking the good in your life and being thankful. The more grateful you are, the more you will attract things that are positive and uplifting. Find the silver lining in the dark cloud. The more you focus on the benefit or lesson, the easier it becomes to see how much you have to be grateful for each and every day! Gratitude carries with it a magickal vibration that can work miracles and light the darkest circumstances.

No matter what is going on in your life, find something to be grateful for, and you will see that vibration expand and bring even more to be thankful for. Gratitude has the power to lift your spirits, increase abundance, and bring joy to your life. Gratitude is transformational. It can change the way you look at your life and the world around you. It is the highest vibration in the universe.

Being grateful for what you have before asking for more is a good way to begin embodying an attitude of gratitude. If you feel down and disappointed with yourself or your life, shift it by being thankful for the things you take for granted every day. How about your ability to breathe? There are those who cannot (think COPD, lung cancer, and emphysema).

If you have to park your car far from the door of a store or restaurant, there is an opportunity to give double thanks—for your ability to walk and for the fact that you own a car that needs parking. Be grateful for the bed you sleep on and the food you eat. Nothing is trivial in the world of gratitude.

Once you begin thinking this way, the day will go much better, your mood will be brighter, and you will shift into an abundance mindset rather than one of lack that results from always wanting more and focusing on what you do not have. When you feel grateful, there is no room for complaining.

One example of a lack mentality is a business owner who has a few clients, but wants many more. Being grateful for the clients there are and making sure they get value from the interactions with the business owner is a good way to cultivate more clients. Yet the likely mindset in this case is, "I only have a few clients." By displaying gratitude for those who are part of the business and making them feel valued, everyone is uplifted, the vibrational frequency is raised, and the likelihood of attracting more ideal clients is increased. Being grateful for every dollar earned increases the abundance frequency and draws more money.

Now you can begin to identify the more subtle modes of gratitude wherein you see the blessing, despite the initial appearance of difficulty, such as being thankful for having:

- A mate to pick up after because in a generally healthy relationship, he or she brings or makes possible certain positive attributes in the relationship, including love and companionship

- A house to clean because you have a roof over your head and the ability to make it your sanctuary

- A job that requires an arduous commute because there is money coming in and being on the road gives you the opportunity to think or to listen to an audio book that normally would not fit into your schedule.

How about gratitude for making a mistake that helped you learn an important lesson? All experiences are valuable, so open your heart with gratitude toward events that on the surface may appear to be negative.

The more gratitude you display, the more things will come into your life to be grateful for. We all have challenges, difficulties, and traumas that enter in at times—it is part of life—but to concentrate on gratitude prevents the problems of life from becoming the ultimate focus.

By being thankful and recognizing the things, people, and circumstances that enrich your life, there will be no end to the blessings you are able to see around you. Life and the part you play in it is an everyday miracle. Embrace it with gratitude and see your life change for the better.

The more you practice gratitude, the brighter the world will be, and the more blessings will be bestowed upon you.

Lesson 8: Stay Open: The Perfect Place at the Perfect Time

Stay open to whatever presents itself and avoid preconceived notions that put the *shoulds* and the *hows* in your way that serve to block your path. Stay open to the possibilities and to the potential held within any given moment. Trust that the Universe knows what it is doing when putting something before you that is new and different. Stay open to what comes and see where it takes you and what you can learn. Every day, there are opportunities to follow a path that you had not considered before. Throw away the agenda and stay open to opportunities that present themselves. The timing is always right because opportunities come when you are ready to receive them.

You are in the perfect place in the perfect time—right here, right now. It may not be aligned with what your mind is telling you should be in your life, but the Universe has positioned you for growth and success by having you experience whatever it is you are going through at the present moment. And the Universe keeps you there for as long as it takes for you to learn what you need to know for the next leg of your journey.

There are times when it seems you have plateaued, that your circumstances have lasted way longer than necessary. You are saying to the Universe, "All right already! I get it!" yet the situation persists. This is reflective of the need to take right action in the situation. It is not merely the need to understand the lesson, but to determine the next task, decision, or strategy that will move you past the hump.

Exercise 5-7: Start by looking at the circumstance and evaluate your thoughts, feelings, and behaviors as they relate to this particular situation. Are you thinking the same thoughts as you always have in regard to what is transpiring? Do you have the same feelings in relation to what is happening? Are you trying the same behaviors as always? If so, then change one or all of these to move past the standstill.

Take a different point of view when considering this condition. Rather than seeing it as right or wrong, good or bad, look at it from an objective, neutral perspective. Remove all of the emotion and see it as though you are a detached third party. Now what do you see? Do you see something that was not readily apparent before? Use this new insight to modify your approach, and the situation will shift for the better.

Additionally, asking the Universe for guidance to move past the impasse and then following the message that comes through will allow faster progress to be made. Check yourself for any resistance to change that may bubble up. It may be that it is not yet time to leave behind the current situation. There may be more to learn and more growth required before moving to the next level. If this is the case, accept it and seek to understand it at a deeper level. While frustrating, it is in your life for a reason.

If you really want things to be different, take note of what the Universe it trying to teach you. There are no random circumstances that occur to punish or inhibit. Even with karma, the situation is there for you to learn and grow, and to put closure to certain relationships and ways of being.

Sometimes you may want to rush your progress, yet obstacles come into your path that prevent you from moving forward. In most cases, the delay will prove beneficial, as you strive to acquire new skills, a new perspective, additional information, or additional interpersonal support. It may be that the roadblock occurs to avoid a detrimental result or aggravation down the road.

By knowing that the Universe acts in the interest of forward motion and believing that everything happens when it is supposed to, it is easier to trust the process of what you are going through and to take advantage of all that is held within the circumstance.

Trust is key—trust in yourself, in the Universe, and in the idea that you cannot see the rationale behind everything that happens. There are forces at work beyond your limited human understanding that reach far afield from what is happening directly in your life. Things need to align on multiple levels, and they will if you stop resisting and go with the flow of the Universe.

Let go of the fear, anxiety, and worry, and tap into the wisdom of the place you are in at this time and in this moment. Release the emotion and open to the guidance that is waiting to be received. What you need in your life is waiting to be shown to you. Use gratitude to enhance your understanding of the magick in this moment.

> "To every thing there is a season, and a time to every
> purpose under the heaven." — Ecclesiastes 3:1 (KJV)

You are always at the perfect place at the perfect time.

Lesson 9: See the Magick: Beliefs Drive Vision

See the magick of creating your ideal future driven by inspired vision and using imagination and experience. Every experience creates a new perspective or adds to an old one. The beliefs you have hold you back or drive you forward. When you decide to establish a new vision, it is important to understand your current beliefs; creating from an old belief system is just a restatement of what you have probably been asking for without getting for years.

Which belief system are you creating from? When was the last time you asked yourself what you truly believe and whether or not it is still valid?

Look at the belief system you follow. How have you been using it? What is your goal in its practice? Are your beliefs true to your nature or are you following the beliefs you grew up with that no longer serve your current identity? What personal insights have you gained as a result of its practice?

Denial of your own nature causes doubt, fear, and worry. It allows others to take you off-center. By understanding your belief system and how it aligns with your core self, you understand your true nature and stand in it in every circumstance. It fosters a closer connection to your inner/intuitive guidance, to creating your life the way you want it to be, and to cultivating healthy relationships with those who support your unique chosen path.

Beliefs drive vision because you cannot see past what you believe. If you believe you will not be successful, then why bother forming a new vision? To build a framework of belief can keep you stuck in the same old patterns. It is possible to construct a completely new framework that suits who you are today. Clear out the old scaffolding that continues to support outmoded beliefs before building anew.

You may not believe it is possible to take a fresh look at yourself or your life, or you may believe that it is really hard to make such significant change. The answer is that it is possible, and that it will require work to do so. Looking at the same problems from the same perspective will not get you anywhere, but with some research, consideration, and help from trusted loved ones or a professional, you can see things differently. Once that happens, a whole new set of possibilities awaken, and a new vision emerges.

It is exhausting to see things the same way over and over and make no progress. Frustration becomes the prominent vibration, and then a giving-up response soon follows. Those who seek enlightenment find it; those who choose to stay mired in old ways of being persist in feeling distraught and restricted.

But as always, you must be ready to see things differently and go in search of new ways of seeing yourself and the world. If you continue the mantra that you do not have the time, nor the money, nor the inclination to do so, then you are not ready. This is exactly the type of mindset that curtails motivation and destroys hope. It is the statement made by those who are comfortable in their discomfort. If you prefer to remain as you are, that is perfectly fine; then give up complaining that you want things to be different. Come to grips with the idea that you really do not want change, and give yourself permission for that to be okay.

There is magick in the world. It is all around you, in nature and in the way your life unfolds. Magick is your ability to create a peaceful, fulfilling life. It is the happiness available to you once you open to it. You are able to see the magick when you are not fighting against anything. You are poised to see it once you let go of the negative, when you are grateful for everything in your life, and when you stay open to seeing joy and infinite possibilities. Using your Inner Magick is how you express your unique gifts and use your natural intuitive sense while flowing with the Divine Essence.

See the magick in everyday miracles; beautiful relationships, how things fall into place "coincidentally," and the effortless way things happen for the highest good—that's when you know you are in the flow of magick.

If you are really ready to make the commitment to create a new vision for your life, then remove all mental and emotional barriers, eliminate perceived obstacles, and start with one simple question: What do I want my life to look like?

Exercise 5-8: To create your ideal life: list all of the things, large and small, that make you happy. Align your life with those things and remove or minimize the things that do not.

Appendix: Dumping, Grounding, & Protecting

In both of my books *The True Nature of Tarot: Your Path to Personal Empowerment* and *The True Nature of Energy: Transforming Anxiety into Tranquility*, there is a chapter on the energetic visualizations of dumping, grounding, and protecting. In case you do not have my other two books, I include it here because these are highly effective ways of ridding yourself of negativity and then refilling with positive energy, followed by divine protection. If you own my other books (thank you!), this is a handy reference. Doing these practices on a regular basis creates a sense of calm and centeredness. It makes you more tolerant of daily annoyances and brightens your energy, all of which contributes to feeling happy.

Clearing and Grounding

Clearing and grounding helps us rid ourselves of toxic energies and feel safe as we go through the day. A general rule of thumb is to ground and protect before starting your day, and then clear and rejuvenate after the day is over.

As we walk through our day and experience life, we collect the energies of others onto our aura, which can make us feel heavy and tired. Grounding is a means of attaching your energy to the Universe and to the Earth, allowing you to feel stable, balanced, and protected. By creating a connection, both above and below, a conduit is formed to allow a steady stream of energy to flow through you. In this way, positive energy flows in from the heavens and negativity flows into the ground. To attach to both is to know an intimate relationship with Source, while experiencing an extraordinary relationship with the planet.

Grounding and energetically protecting yourself before heading out for the day ensures a calmer overall experience, with less impact from external energies. Initially set aside ten to fifteen minutes in the morning to do the following exercise. With practice, you will be able to do it in half the time. You can perform this technique inside or outside.

Start by closing your eyes and imagining tubes descending from the bottom of your feet and moving downward through the floor, the ground, the layers of the earth, and into its core of molten orange light. Begin to pull the orange light into the tubes and up through the layers of the earth, the ground, the floor, and into the bottoms of your feet.

Continue to pull the bright orange light up through your legs, into your torso, and up into your head. Feel the bright orange light filling your body and the strength it brings. Take as much as you need. You are tapped into an unlimited resource when you are plugged into the earth's center. When you feel filled to capacity, stop pulling the orange light, but do not disconnect from the earth. This will help you to maintain a firmly planted feeling as you move throughout the day. You are now grounded from below.

Next is to protect from above. Picture a large column of bright white light coming down from the heavens and pouring down around your entire body. Imagine being coated in this light from your head to your feet. Envision the light as a solid around your body. Make sure all parts of you are covered. Now encase the white light with a thin, solid border of bright blue light. Beam the light out as far as you can.

Choose targets for the light to hit, such as trees on either side and in front and back of you. If indoors, beam your light from wall to wall, side to side, front to back. Focus on making it brighter and wider. Now you are completely grounded and protected.

With practice, you will be able to perform this grounding method faster and more effectively. Try beaming the white light farther out each time, until you are able to touch objects several feet away all around you. If done correctly, you will feel energized, calm, stable, and ready to face whatever the day may bring.

External energies are one source of harmonic dissonance within the personal energy field known as the aura. Our own thoughts and emotions are a source of discordant energies, as well. Keeping yourself clear of your own negative thoughts and emotions is essential to raising your vibrational level and to increasing the amount of energy available to you. By regularly clearing your energetic field and grounding, you will feel stronger and more tolerant of the energies around you.

Clearing your energy serves to rid yourself of internal and external unwanted energies.

Dumping these energies after a long day will make you feel lighter and energized. I recommend going outside and standing on a patch of ground (not concrete) to perform this exercise.

Close your eyes and take a few deep breaths. Start at your head and take all of the negative thoughts that swirl around, all the doubts about yourself and your life, and all of the self-deprecating statements you make on a regular basis. Accumulate them in a ball and allow them to drain from your head and down your neck.

At the throat, take all of the things you wish you had said and all of the things you wish you had not said, and combine them with the negative thoughts. Let all of these flow into your chest where your emotions live, and let go of all the pain, hurt, and disappointment you have experienced in your relationships. These heavy energies are now mingled with the negativity from your head and throat.

Move them together into your stomach, where they accumulate with the dense vibrations of stress and fear. Allow yourself to release these altogether and let them flow down your legs, out the bottoms of your feet, and into the ground. Allow all the stress of the day, your worry, doubt, and fear to drain from your body, starting at the head and moving all the way down your arms, your torso, your legs, and out the bottoms of your feet. Let the negative energy flow into the ground (Mother Earth will cleanse it) until there is nothing left.

When you feel empty, open your eyes. Look around you. After performing this dumping exercise, all of my clients report either a profound clarity of their physical vision, that the trees look closer and more vivid, or an intense lightness of being, like a huge weight has been lifted.

After dumping all of those dense vibrations, it is important immediately and intentionally to fill yourself with clean Earth energy to avoid random energies entering you. Move about ten feet from where you dumped the negativity and stand on a fresh patch of ground. Send your roots out from the bottoms of your feet into the core of the earth and pull up fresh energy, bright, orange light that flows up the roots and into your feet, up your legs, and torso.

At your chest, mix the bright orange light with bright green energy for growth, health, and development. Envision is swirling in your chest, down your arms, and into your head. Feel the elation that this fresh energy contains, and allow it to fill and rejuvenate you. Continue to allow this new energy to flow until you feel full.

Another method for clearing the energies of the day is to take a shower and use a sea salt scrub with lavender or take a hot bath with lavender sea salts. As you bathe, picture all frustrations, annoyances, and disappointments leaving you and pouring down the drain along with the dirty water. This method provides a good transition from the work day into a calm evening with loved ones.

Performing clearing exercises at least several times a week is recommended. For times of unusually high stress, it may be appropriate to do one of these methods at the end of each day. When feeling agitated, restless, or tense, or even to maintain your center, get out into nature. Natural environments clear and strengthen the aura and provide vibrant surroundings to enjoy.

The type of natural environment is a personal choice. Many of my clients and students enjoy being around the ocean and letting the sound of crashing waves, the call of the seagulls, and the smell of the salt air cleanse and calm them. My favorite natural environment is the forest. The earthy fragrance, the scurrying of chipmunks and squirrels, and the seasonal changes of the trees make me feel peaceful and radiant. As I walk, I attach my auric field to the trees on either side of the path, allowing me to pull in fresh energy while dumping negative or stale energy into the earth through my feet. With each step, energy blocks are eliminated and replaced with the vital green energy of the trees. The woods encourage my chakras or energy centers to open wider to accept the life force of the trees. The volume of positive energy flowing into me pushes away negativity and allows the light to flourish within me.

Glossary

Anxiety Death Spiral—Anxiety is triggered by a particular situation and then exacerbated by the barrage of negative automatic thoughts that deepen the anxiety toward a panic response. For example, anxiety from being late for work is heightened by thoughts of embarrassment, disappointing others, losing credibility, or getting fired, with each step more intense than the next. This creates intense anxiety that results in physical and emotional distress.

Aura—The distinctive energy field or essence that surrounds a person, place, or thing.

Chakra—Energy centers of the body, usually considered seven in number. When open, energy flows easily; when closed, the person experiences discomfort, illness, or stagnation.

Divine/Spirit/Universe—A general term to describe whatever higher power/spiritual presence the individual relates to.

Divine Downloads—Intuitive guidance in the form of messages that come from connecting to Spirit.

Divine Essence—The spiritual energy that flows in and around all people, places, and things, connecting them and making them one.

Four-Part Inner Guidance System—You have a four-part inner guidance system that tells you when you are making decisions that are in alignment with your highest good. Start by checking in with your body's reactions as we discussed earlier in this chapter. Then check in with your emotions. Think about your options one by one. Do you feel excited, happy, or upset? Check in mentally. Does your mind go to all of the problems that may arise as a result of a particular choice, or does it embrace all of the potential and possibilities that may present themselves? Finally, check in spiritually. "Ask" Source whether this is the right direction or choice. Is it for your highest good? Go with the first impression that comes through. It may be a simple yes or no response. If nothing comes through, ask for a sign. The answer may come later in the day or later in the week, but as long as you pose the question, you will get an answer.

Clearing and Grounding—Clearing and grounding helps us rid ourselves of toxic energies and feel safe as we go through the day. A general rule of thumb is to ground and protect before starting your day, and then clear and rejuvenate after the day is over.

Highest Good—Resulting in the best possible outcome to create ultimate harmony and balance.

High Service—While serving others, you also honor and serve yourself. You do not work to your detriment, to your exhaustion and frustration, but rather, in the helping, you are energized, peaceful, and harmonious. Many times it comes in the form of expressing your purpose and unique gifts to serve and support others.

Inner Magick—A term used to refer to the intuitive abilities and unique gifts that everyone possesses. It differs from magic with a "c" in that magick refers to the realm of the illusionist. You are the Magician, orchestrating and creating your life in accordance with your true self. Coming into your power gives a sense of security and purpose that promotes personal responsibility and attainment of your true potential. Inner Magick allows you to become more secure within yourself and more accepting of others.

Use my formulary to unlock your Inner Magick:

Fear = worry + doubt - vulnerability - courage

Will = mind control + self-discipline + fortitude

Wisdom = knowledge + experience + application

Self-mastery = will + clarity + focus + wisdom - fear

True power, the real magick, is hidden within you. That is why true magick and its practice is based in self-knowledge, the development of personal will, and connection to the Divine Will, which allows you to have the confidence to create your life any way you choose. In all tales of magick, seekers are required to overcome personal challenges, let go of behaviors and beliefs that block them, and get rid of fear, doubt, and worry in order to release their Inner Magick. They have to trust themselves and open to their intuitive guidance. Essentially, they have to get out of their own way. They possess magickal ability, but they cannot come fully into their power until they make significant changes within themselves. The same is true for you. With each layer of blockage that is removed, your power rises closer to the surface and you are able to release your Inner Magick.

Magick—The common spelling of Magic with a "c" refers to entertainment, hiding the truth, or trickery, whereas Magick with a "k" is a path to enlightenment and a means to transform our reality through changes in perspective and perception. It reveals to us the true nature of reality, allows us to get closer to the Divine, and to understand ourselves at a deep level.

Right Action—Acting in harmony with yourself and in alignment with the path you seek.

Wishcraft—Saying what you want over and over again in hopes that it comes true or until you start to believe it to be true.

References

Blum, R. (1993). *The book of runes: A handbook for the use of an ancient oracle, the Viking Runes.* New York: St. Martin's Press.

Duncker, K. (1945). *On problem-solving.* Washington, D.C: American Psychological Association.

Kirste, I., Nicola, Z., Kronenberg, G., Walker, T. L., Liu, R. C., & Kempermann, G. (2013). Is silence golden? Effects of auditory stimuli and their absence on adult hippocampal neurogenesis. *Brain Structure and Function, 220*(2), 1221-1228. doi:10.1007/s00429-013-0679-3

Scholl, B., Gao, X., & Wehr, M. (2010). Nonoverlapping Sets of Synapses Drive On Responses and Off Responses in Auditory Cortex. *Neuron, 65*(3), 412-421. doi:10.1016/j.neuron.2010.01.020

Wing, D. (2013). *The true nature of energy: Transforming anxiety into tranquility.* Ann Arbor: Marvelous Spirit Press.

Wing, D. (2010). *The true nature of tarot: Your path to personal empowerment.* Ann Arbor, MI: Marvelous Spirit Press.

Bibliography

Anderson, J. R. (1980). *Cognitive psychology and its implications.* San Francisco: W.H. Freeman.

Gawain, S., & King, L. (1986). *Living in the light.* Mill Valley, CA: Whatever Pub.

Hawkins, D. R. (2002). *The eye of the I.* W. Sedona, AZ: Veritas.

Heidegger, M. (1988). *Hegel's Phenomenology of spirit.* Bloomington: Indiana University Press.

Initiates, T. (2008). *The Kybalion: A study of the hermetic philosophy of ancient Egypt and Greece.* New York: Jeremy P. Tarcher/Penguin.

Kelly, G. A. (1963). *A theory of personality: The psychology of personal constructs.* New York.

Maltz, M. (1960). *Psycho-cybernetics: A new way to get more living out of life.* Englewood Cliffs, NJ: Prentice-Hall.

Merleau-Ponty, M. (n.d.). *Phenomenology of perception.*

Myss, C. M. (1997). *Why people don't heal and how they can.* New York: Harmony Books.

Neville., & Neville. (2012). *The power of awareness.* New York: Jeremy P. Tarcher/Penguin.

Rudhyar, D. (1972). *The astrological houses; the spectrum of individual experience.* Garden City, NY: Doubleday.

Shinn, F. S. (2010). *The wisdom of Florence Scovel Shinn.* Charleston, SC: SoHo Books.

About the Author

Author, teacher, personal transformation guide, and intuitive consultant Diane Wing, M.A. enjoys exploring the mysteries of life and the way that people experience themselves and the world around them. A phenomenologist at the core, Diane uses a variety of techniques combined with discovering unique patterns experienced by her clients to reveal a deeper understanding of the self and to shift their perspective enabling them to move past obstacles that keep them stuck.

Diane Wing is dedicated to helping people get grounded and trust themselves, so they can live a peaceful and fulfilling life of joyful self-expression. She inspires others and teaches them to safely tap into the energies around them to turn anxiety into tranquility. Her clients are those who are ready to stop struggling in their personal life so they can feel their best.

Wing sees connections between things that seem disparate to others and can help you see their significance in your life. She's an idea person who helps you shift your perspective to see yourself and your life in a whole new way and is a master at bringing magick into the everyday. She wants to live in a world where people feel inspired and motivated to evolve beyond their current way of being. As a Perspective Changer and Blockage Buster, she's a wiz at helping people find their Inner Magick to help them be happy in the present while creating their ideal future.

To that end, Diane Wing created a body of work focused on knowing the self at a deep level in order to build self-trust and self-confidence. Her books, both dark fantasy fiction and enlightening non-fiction, hold lessons based in Universal and Magickal Law and energetic consciousness. Her games, Pathways and Insight Stones®, are systems of metaphysics designed to facilitate self-discovery, develop intuitive ability, and to enhance self-awareness. The emphasis of her school, Wing Academy of Unfoldment, and of her radio show, Wing Academy Radio, helps students and listeners learn ways to take metaphysical and personal development concepts and apply them to everyday life in their own distinct way. It's about going deeper and seeing the patterns of your life.

Wing's books create a transformational experience for the reader while incorporating a bit of the unexpected. Many say that her fiction has a sense of Karmic justice rendered within the realm of the unknown and that her non-fiction brings about a heightened awareness of the self and the world to enhance understanding of our own internal transformations.

According to Diane Wing, "Ever since I was little, the world felt magic-kal. [Magick with a "k" is used to differentiate the magic of an illusionist or stage magician from the magick that includes your intuitive abilities and tapping into the flow of the Universe). The world was beautiful and mysterious, filled with things to learn and experience. The path led me to become a lifetime student of metaphysics, mysticism, magick, and spirit-uality and to achieve a Master's degree in psychology... and it all shows up in my writing. You never know what's waiting around the bend.

"The world still feels magickal to me; every act of nature, every ener-getic exchange, every new discovery is perceived through the eyes of wonder. I now understand that self-knowledge is the key to all magickal operations; the discovery of our own Inner Magick is essential to living in concert with the Universe. We are the Magician, as in tarot, orchestrating and creating life in accordance with our true self."

Diane is an avid reader, bibliophile, lover of trees, and a lifelong learner. She and her husband are pet parents to a sweet little Shih Tzu.

Find out more and listen to Wing Academy Radio at www.DianeWing.com

Index

Gain a Fresh Perspective Using the Energies Around You

Have you ever walked into a room and felt like you wanted to leave right away? Ever met a person for whom you had an instant dislike for no apparent reason? Been around certain people and suddenly feel exhausted? People, animals, situations, objects, and environments contain and give off energy.

The energies within and around you can be a major source of anxiety. To discover how to observe, interpret, and direct this abundant energy is to harness the power at your fingertips and create tranquility in your life. This book can guide you in that discovery.

In *The True Nature of Energy*, you will:

- Improve your relationship with yourself and others
- Remove unnecessary emotions and see more objectively
- Attract the right people and circumstances
- Clear old, outmoded energies from your life
- Increase self-trust, self-esteem, and self-confidence
- Learn to sense and direct the energies around you
- Enhance your natural intuitive ability
- Find out your vibrational level by taking the Wing Vibrational Scale Quiz
- Learn simple techniques to fully take charge of your life and your destiny.

From Marvelous Spirit Press

ISBN-978-1-61599-196-9

CPSIA information can be obtained
at www.ICGtesting.com
Printed in the USA
BVHW042116251218
536372BV00006B/113/P